*R*ecasting the Text

Recasting the Text

*I*nquiry-Based Activities for Comprehending and Composing

Fran Claggett
Louann Reid
Ruth Vinz

Boynton/Cook Publishers
Heinemann
Portsmouth, NH

Boynton/Cook Publishers
A subsidiary of Reed Elsevier Inc.
361 Hanover Street
Portsmouth, NH 03801-3912
Offices and agents throughout the world

Editor: Peter Stillman
Manufacturing: Louise Richardson
Cover photo: Renée M. Nicholls
Cover design: Joanne Tranchemontagne and Renée M. Nicholls

The authors and publisher wish to thank those who have generously given permission to reprint material:
Pages 6, 7, 8, 9, 11, 13, 15: "To a Friend Whose Work Has Come to Triumph" from ALL MY PRETTY ONES by Anne Sexton. Copyright © 1962 by Anne Sexton, renewed 1990 by Linda G. Sexton. First published in *The Nation*. Reprinted by permission of Houghton Mifflin Co. All rights reserved.
Page 10: "The Starry Night" from ALL MY PRETTY ONES by Anne Sexton. Copyright © 1962 by Anne Sexton, renewed 1990 by Linda G. Sexton. First published in *The Nation*. Reprinted by permission of Houghton Mifflin Co. All rights reserved.
(Credit lines continued at the end of the book.)

Claggett, Mary Frances.
    Recasting the text : inquiry-based activities for comprehending and composing / Fran Claggett, Louann Reid, Ruth Vinz.
        p.   cm.
    Includes bibliographical references and index.
    ISBN 0-86709-402-8
    1. Reading (Secondary)   2. Reading comprehension.   3. English language—Composition and exercises—Study and teaching (Secondary)
I. Reid, Louann.   II. Vinz, Ruth.   III. Title.
LB1632.C54   1996
428.4'0712—dc20   96-24629
                                                            CIP

Printed in the United States of America on acid-free paper
99 98 97 96   DA   1 2 3 4 5 6 7 8 9

Contents

Preface

Recasting the Text: Inquiry-Based Activities for Comprehending and Composing provides activities that help you explore multiple ways of reading and recreating a text in various forms. Examining works from diverse times, places, and peoples, you will see how individuals reread and re-see human experience through stories. You will gain perspectives that enrich your understanding of these recastings and will write many of your own transformations as well.

More or less obviously, a textbook reflects the values and beliefs of its authors. This text is no different. We value close reading of literature and careful attention to craft in the writing of literature. Yet, in many other ways, the book you're reading now does differ from the huge anthologies currently available.

Our overriding goal is to help you become transactive, discerning readers and thoughtful, perceptive writers. The way to approach this ideal, we decided, is by integrating the language arts as fully as possible. In this text, we consciously draw on many ways of learning that we have found useful to our students—observing, analyzing, imagining, and reflecting. Thus you'll find language and literature experiences structured so that you use writing, drawing, performing, and discussing to learn about what you're reading.

We believe that you as a reader need to find something of yourself in every selection, defining yourself as you examine the text. We also believe that through the shared stories and poems you read and write you will develop your understanding of how stories form and are transformed by human experience. This book offers texts from a variety of times and places written by professionals and students.

As you read and write, listen and speak, perform and draw, you will employ several language tools. Logs are a vital means for responding to the text. In logs and more sustained projects and papers, you are continually directed to extend your thinking beyond response and to engage in analysis, evaluation, and reflection. Performing and drawing are also powerful ways to read and interpret literature. Finally we give you guidelines for developing a portfolio that includes work completed in various media while using this textbook.

More and more teachers have expressed a need to accommodate various learning styles, provide opportunities for collaboration on problem-solving projects, and help you engage in a real negotiation with texts in both reading and writing. This book is designed to meet those needs.

Acknowledgments

We wish to thank our colleagues who have contributed to this text by engaging with us in the ongoing dialogue, the "grand conversation" about teaching and learning. Their names are too numerous to mention, but they extend from California to Florida, from New York to Colorado, from Idaho to Georgia, and points in between. We also wish to thank the many students whose patience and enthusiasm led us to refinements in our design of better ways to help them excel in and enjoy the processes of comprehending and composing. A special thanks goes to those students whose work appears in these pages.

Particular mention must go to Scott Lindsten and Juhl Wojahn, who carefully transcribed student work; to Jean Wendelin, who patiently tracked down difficult sources for permission to reprint works; and to Judith Hargrave, whose close reading and diligent copyediting ensured completion of the final manuscript. We are grateful to Madge Holland for reading and rereading the text, always with an eye toward clarity and classroom usefulness.

No acknowledgments would be complete without mentioning the work of those researchers and thinkers whose work has so powerfully affected our thinking about teaching and learning. Of most immediate relevance to this book is Louise M. Rosenblatt, for her seminal work with a transactional approach to reading and writing. Jimmy Britton's vision played a vital role in our understanding of language and learning. The thinking and writing of John Mayher, Dan Kirby, Robert Scholes, and Bob Probst are also implicated in the concepts and projects that we present in this text.

Finally we want to thank Bob Boynton and Peter Stillman for envisioning and trusting that there were books that *should* be written—books that depart from the standard fare available to both teachers and students. They have questioned, provoked, and supported us through all of the stages that led to the publication of *Recasting the Text.*

1

Exploring the
Possibilities:
An Introduction

*W*e've titled this book *Recasting the Text* deliberately because we think it is important for you to explore many different ways of reading a piece of literature. Reading means more than opening a book, moving your eyes across a page, and trying to figure out what the author means. *Reading,* as we use the word, involves using all of your knowledge and experience as you work out your interpretation of a story, poem, play, or essay. There are many ways to read a book, just as there are many ways to read the world. *Reading* involves more than understanding words: We talk about reading the weather, reading other people's moods, reading a friend's actions or a parent's tone of voice.

To help you expand and extend your abilities as a reader, you will use the activities in this book to recast some of the works, sometimes taking the role of secondary author. You will rewrite some texts from different points of view, explore how certain choices affect the meaning, and then become the author and make different choices.

We use the word *text* often throughout this book, and for us, text means a poem, play, novel, short story, diary entry, essay, letter, film, drawing, painting—nearly anything that requires reading. Text is an artifact of imagining and crafting, something you or someone else creates. The text is like a fabric of many colors or textures with each reader taking a different thread or color of meaning from what's said and not said. In this book, we'll introduce ways that you can step back from the words of a text and look through a variety of lenses and from different angles. Each lens and angle will give you different ways of thinking about the reading.

Other people will read a text differently from the ways you read it. That's one reason we ask you to respond to what you read and then to share your ideas and collaborate with other readers to make comparisons. You will need to listen carefully to one another and be sensitive to why and how your meanings differ. Your experiences with family and friends or in your school or community will influence how you sort through and make sense of the experiences you find in literature. For example, if you've just experienced the loss of a close friend, you might respond deeply to a story about separation. In short, pay attention. Listen. Question. Keep an open mind. Share your thinking with others. Your class is a community of readers, and it is important to hear different opinions. Remember that while there is no "right" interpretation, you do need to validate your interpretation. It must make sense in light of the text itself, and it must make sense to you, given your own experience and knowledge. The meaning of what you read is what happens between you, the community of readers, and the text.

As you work on the projects in this book, you will explore different ways of seeing, what we call *angles of vision*. Looking at a text from a number of different angles, you'll find multiple ways of understanding it. What are these angles of vision? You might write or draw how you feel after you finish a story or poem; you might tell the story to someone who hasn't read it; you might tell your group about an experience of your own that was similar to what you read and listen to their experiences; or you might write a poem or story of your own. You might read more stories or poems by the same author, or you might reread the story or poem. All of these responses will help you come to your understanding of a text.

We begin by asking you to look at a poem from seven different angles of vision (see pages 6–15). We chose a poem for practice because it is short, although these angles work with all kinds of texts. The angles we suggest are not the only ways of looking at a text; there are many others that you'll find by yourself or with your discussion group. We won't be asking you to explore all of these angles for every text that you read, but we will always ask you to look at the text from more than one angle. There is no particular order to these angles, except for the first—the personal response—and the last, when we ask you to move back from the text and reflect on its larger meanings.

As you work through the activities in this book, you will discover that we ask you to use many kinds of writing as you move from developing your interpretations of texts to crafting your own ideas into stories, poems, and reflective essays. As you work through the activities, you'll be asked to select some of your drafts and revise (or "re-vision") them into finished pieces for your portfolio, a collection of your best work.

*T*erms and Concepts You Need to Know

Following are some of the terms and concepts that we use frequently throughout this book:

Log: The log is where you'll record ongoing work for a particular project. The log may include responses to or discussions about the texts you read. It may include specific observation assignments or lists generated from brainstorming. The form should fit the purposes for using the log. Your teacher may prefer one kind of log—such as a loose-leaf notebook. Other teachers may prefer spiral notebooks.

In this book, we have numbered the log entries by chapter. When you begin a new chapter, label the new set of log entries with the name of that chapter and begin numbering again with Log Entry 1.

Double-entry Log: There will be some times that we will ask you to set up your log as a double-entry notebook (sometimes called a dual-entry notebook), recording on the left-hand side of the page the words, phrases, or lines that trigger a response for you. On the right-hand side, write your own thoughts and ideas. Set up your log this way:

Double-entry Log Format

Class _____	Name _____
Date _____	Log Entry # _____
Words, phrases, or lines from the text	*My response to the text*

Clustering: Clustering is a process that helps you generate ideas and explore possibilities for writing. It is similar to what you might know as "webbing" or "semantic mapping." Begin by writing the key or stimulus word in the center of a page; then, in two or three minutes, write as many words and phrases as you can, radiating outward from the key word. Each word or phrase triggers another until you have a web of words and phrases. Usually you find, as you are clustering, that ideas you were not even aware of emerge from the web.

Mapping: Mapping is a more consciously organized way of arranging your ideas on a page than clustering. In mapping, you begin with some ideas or categories and place your items of information meaningfully on the page. The way you organize your material makes it available to you visually. Notes that would take pages, for example, can all be placed on a one-page map. Maps may be completely made up of words; they may use words and symbols or drawings; or they may be completely nonverbal—all symbols and drawings.

Graphic: A graphic is a drawing, cluster, or map. We'll often ask you to respond to or interpret a piece of literature by drawing or mapping your ideas.

Partner or Group: Throughout the book, we will frequently ask you to collaborate with a partner or a small group of your classmates as you explore your understanding of a text and work through revisions in your own writing or performing. Your teacher will establish these groups; they may change from time to time, depending on how your teacher organizes the class.

Writing Folder: The writing folder is a place to keep your work in progress—drafts of essays, stories, and poems. When you work through a particular assignment—writing a draft, having your writing group respond to it and, possibly, revising it—you will keep all of that work in your writing folder.

Course Portfolio: The portfolio represents your best completed work. When you have a finished piece of work, one that your teacher has read and responded to and that you have revised, put that piece into your portfolio. Throughout this book, we suggest many activities that could lead to finished portfolio pieces. Each is identified in the text as a *portfolio entry*.

Angles of Vision on a Poem

To demonstrate how various readings and perspectives can contribute to the meanings we make from text, we ask you now to look from seven different angles of vision at a poem about the myth of Icarus. Because we want you to respond first to the poem itself, we omit the poet's name until the fourth angle.

Remember that this is practice, to acquaint you with the strategies you will develop as you read and write your way through *Recasting the Text*. To work through these angles, you will need to set up a log. Your teacher will assign or have you choose a partner for collaborating. Begin by reading the poem; then follow directions for each of the seven angles of vision. You will not read other works this many times, but we hope experimenting with these angles of vision will help you explore possibilities for your work with other selections in this book.

Angle 1: Initial Responses

To a Friend Whose Work Has Come to Triumph

Consider Icarus, pasting those sticky wings on,
testing that strange little tug at his shoulder blade,
and think of that first flawless moment over the lawn
of the labyrinth. Think of the difference it made!
There below are the trees, as awkward as camels;
and here are the shocked starlings pumping past
and think of innocent Icarus who is doing quite well:
larger than a sail, over the fog and the blast
of the plushy ocean, he goes. Admire his wings!
Feel the fire at his neck and see how casually
he glances up and is caught, wondrously tunneling
into that hot eye. Who cares that he fell back to the sea?
See him acclaiming the sun and come plunging down
while his sensible daddy goes straight into town.

Log Entry 1

Consider Icarus; consider this poem. What are your thoughts, feelings, observations, or questions? Use drawings and/or words to express your initial responses.

Collaborating

Share what you have written or drawn with a partner.

Angle 2: Story Threads

To a Friend Whose Work Has Come to Triumph

Consider Icarus, pasting those sticky wings on,
testing that strange little tug at his shoulder blade,
and think of that first flawless moment over the lawn
of the labyrinth. Think of the difference it made!
There below are the trees, as awkward as camels;
and here are the shocked starlings pumping past
and think of innocent Icarus who is doing quite well:
larger than a sail, over the fog and the blast
of the plushy ocean, he goes. Admire his wings!
Feel the fire at his neck and see how casually
he glances up and is caught, wondrously tunneling
into that hot eye. Who cares that he fell back to the sea?
See him acclaiming the sun and come plunging down
while his sensible daddy goes straight into town.

*C*ollaborating

- Share any information you have about Icarus with a partner. Who was he? What did he do? Are there any stories you remember reading about him?

- Turn to page 74 and read the story of Daedalus and Icarus. Talk about how knowing the myth affects your understanding of the poem.

- Share any stories from your own experience that the Icarus story makes you think of.

*L*og Entry 2

In a cluster or a drawing, trace the threads or similarities that connect your stories with the story of Icarus.

Angle 3: Shifting Perspectives

To a Friend Whose Work Has Come to Triumph

Consider Icarus, pasting those sticky wings on,
testing that strange little tug at his shoulder blade,
and think of that first flawless moment over the lawn
of the labyrinth. Think of the difference it made!
There below are the trees, as awkward as camels;
and here are the shocked starlings pumping past
and think of innocent Icarus who is doing quite well:
larger than a sail, over the fog and the blast
of the plushy ocean, he goes. Admire his wings!
Feel the fire at his neck and see how casually
he glances up and is caught, wondrously tunneling
into that hot eye. Who cares that he fell back to the sea?
See him acclaiming the sun and come plunging down
while his sensible daddy goes straight into town.

Collaborating

One of the ways to read a piece of literature is to play "what if" and speculate about alternatives. For example, in focusing on the meaning of the title of a work, you might consider how different titles would change the meaning of the poem for you. Speculating on "what if" often leads you to consider possible interpretations.

Speculate with your partner on how you might read this poem differently if . . .

- the title were "Light," "Expectations," or "Greed." What other title would fit this poem? How would this different title affect the poem's meaning for you? How do you explain the title the poet chose?

- Icarus were a story of a mother and a daughter. How would that affect your understanding or your feelings about the poem?

- you were a parent who had lost a child because of the child's daring bravado (flying too near the sun). How do you think your experience would affect your understanding of the poem?

Log Entry 3

Write up the speculation you are interested in exploring in more detail or the one that most intrigues you.

Angle 4: Connecting with the Writer

To a Friend Whose Work Has Come to Triumph

Anne Sexton

Consider Icarus, pasting those sticky wings on,
testing that strange little tug at his shoulder blade,
and think of that first flawless moment over the lawn
of the labyrinth. Think of the difference it made!
There below are the trees, as awkward as camels;
and here are the shocked starlings pumping past
and think of innocent Icarus who is doing quite well:
larger than a sail, over the fog and the blast
of the plushy ocean, he goes. Admire his wings!
Feel the fire at his neck and see how casually
he glances up and is caught, wondrously tunneling
into that hot eye. Who cares that he fell back to the sea?
See him acclaiming the sun and come plunging down
while his sensible daddy goes straight into town.

Anne Sexton's life has been the subject of intense scrutiny. She began to write seriously while she was recovering from a mental breakdown. She called it a "rebirth at twenty-nine." The power of her poems was soon recognized by the poetry community, and she was awarded the Pulitzer Prize for her book *Transformations,* a series of powerful retellings of Grimm's fairy tales. Her poems are often brutally frank about her own life, which was tumultuous in its emotional swings. At the age of forty-six, she committed suicide, leaving a husband and two daughters.

Maxine Kumin, another noted poet, encouraged Sexton in her early days of writing and remained a close personal and professional confidante. After Sexton's death, Kumin wrote about how they always shared their poems on the telephone. Following is a brief extract from Kumin's reminiscences titled *A Friendship Remembered.*

> Early on in our friendship, indeed almost as soon as we began to share poems, we began to share them on the telephone. . . . We both installed second phone lines in our houses so that the rest of each of our families—the two husbands, the five children—could have equal access to a phone and we could talk privately for as long as we wanted. I confess we sometimes connected with a phone call and kept that line linked for hours at a stretch, interrupting poem-talk to stir the spaghetti sauce, switch the laundry, or try out a new image on the typewriter; we whistled into the receiver to each other when we were ready to resume. It worked wonders.
>
> Writing poems and bouncing them off each other by phone does develop the ear. You learn to hear line breaks, to pick up and be critical of unintended internal rhyme, or intended slant rhyme or whatever.

Anne Sexton's poem "The Starry Night," like "To a Friend Whose Work Has Come to Triumph," takes its genesis from a reference to another work, in this case a painting by Vincent Van Gogh. As with the first poem, the allusion to the painting in this poem is a springboard for personal reflections on life and death.

The Starry Night
Anne Sexton

That does not keep me from having a terrible need of—shall I say the word—religion. Then I go out at night to paint the stars.
(Vincent Van Gogh in a letter to his brother)

The town does not exist
except where one black-haired tree slips
up like a drowned woman into the hot sky.
The town is silent. The night boils with eleven stars.
Oh starry starry night! This is how
I want to die.

It moves. They are all alive.
Even the moon bulges in its orange irons
to push children, like a god, from its eye.
The old unseen serpent swallows up the stars.
Oh starry starry night! This is how
I want to die:

into that rushing beast of the night,
sucked up by that great dragon, to split
from my life with no flag,
no belly,
no cry.

Collaborating

Discuss with your partner how knowing some details about Anne Sexton affects your understanding of her poems. Following are some questions to get you started in your discussion:

- How does the fact that Sexton committed suicide affect your understanding of "The Starry Night"? Of "To a Friend Whose Work Has Come to Triumph"?

- How does reading "The Starry Night" affect your reading of "To a Friend Whose Work Has Come to Triumph"?

- How do Maxine Kumin's comments affect your understanding of "To a Friend Whose Work Has Come to Triumph"? Of "The Starry Night"? Of Anne Sexton's life?

Log Entry 4

Describe how your earlier readings of "To a Friend Whose Work Has Come to Triumph" have been affected by the biographical information, "The Starry Night," and your discussion.

Angle 5: Language and Craft

To a Friend Whose Work Has Come to Triumph
Anne Sexton

Consider Icarus, pasting those sticky wings on,
testing that strange little tug at his shoulder blade,
and think of that first flawless moment over the lawn

of the labyrinth. Think of the difference it made!
There below are the trees, as awkward as camels;
and here are the shocked starlings pumping past
and think of innocent Icarus who is doing quite well:
larger than a sail, over the fog and the blast
of the plushy ocean, he goes. Admire his wings!
Feel the fire at his neck and see how casually
he glances up and is caught, wondrously tunneling
into that hot eye. Who cares that he fell back to the sea?
See him acclaiming the sun and come plunging down
while his sensible daddy goes straight into town.

Poetry comes in many forms. Some forms are very loose, while others are structured in such matters as line length, rhythm, and rhyme patterns. Maxine Kumin told us that Anne Sexton worked with very tight forms in many of her poems. If you have studied the forms of poetry, you may have noticed that "To a Friend Whose Work Has Come to Triumph" observes the pattern of a sonnet.

Collaborating

Talk with your partner about which words and phrases you find interesting in "To a Friend Whose Work Has Come to Triumph." Are the phrases you selected ones that you like because of the sound? Because of the way they make you think or feel? Because of other reasons?

Log Entry 5

Using a dual-entry format (two columns), jot down in the left-hand column the interesting words and phrases you selected. In the right-hand column, write a few words explaining why you chose each one.

Collaborating

Talk with your partner and then the whole class about the following questions:

- Reread the poem and discuss any repetitions of sounds, both within lines and at the ends of lines. How do these repetitions affect your understanding?

- What other elements of form do you find in "To a Friend Whose Work Has Come to Triumph"?

- In what ways can knowing the form of a poem help you as you read it?

- Why do you think a poet would choose a form as precise as a sonnet?

Log Entry 5 (continued)

Record in your log the highlights of your discussions with your partner and with the class about form, including how the form of this poem affects your understanding or enjoyment.

Angle 6: Recasting the Text

To a Friend Whose Work Has Come to Triumph
Anne Sexton

Consider Icarus, pasting those sticky wings on,
testing that strange little tug at his shoulder blade,
and think of that first flawless moment over the lawn
of the labyrinth. Think of the difference it made!
There below are the trees, as awkward as camels;

and here are the shocked starlings pumping past
and think of innocent Icarus who is doing quite well:
larger than a sail, over the fog and the blast
of the plushy ocean, he goes. Admire his wings!
Feel the fire at his neck and see how casually
he glances up and is caught, wondrously tunneling
into that hot eye. Who cares that he fell back to the sea?
See him acclaiming the sun and come plunging down
while his sensible daddy goes straight into town.

Literature is filled with what we call *recastings*. These recastings may take many forms: Writers may retell the original so that a story takes place in a different time period, to different people. Writers may change the form from a story to a play, for example, or from a painting to a poem, as Sexton does in "The Starry Night."

"To a Friend Whose Work Has Come to Triumph," as you already know, is itself a recasting of an old story, the Greek myth of Daedalus and Icarus. This particular story has been recast many times, in paintings as well as in poems. Later in this book, you will read four additional Icarus poems.

*Lo*g Entry 6

Try your hand at recasting this poem in any of the following ways:

- as a drawing

- as another poem

- as a dialogue between Icarus and a friend of his

- as a conversation between a father and son or between a mother and a daughter (or make up your own relationship for the dialogue)

- as a work that uses your own structure and form for recasting

Angle 7: You, the Text, the World

To a Friend Whose Work Has Come to Triumph
Anne Sexton

Consider Icarus, pasting those sticky wings on,
testing that strange little tug at his shoulder blade,
and think of that first flawless moment over the lawn
of the labyrinth. Think of the difference it made!
There below are the trees, as awkward as camels;
and here are the shocked starlings pumping past
and think of innocent Icarus who is doing quite well:
larger than a sail, over the fog and the blast
of the plushy ocean, he goes. Admire his wings!
Feel the fire at his neck and see how casually
he glances up and is caught, wondrously tunneling
into that hot eye. Who cares that he fell back to the sea?
See him acclaiming the sun and come plunging down
while his sensible daddy goes straight into town.

We hope that this close study of "To a Friend Whose Work Has Come to Triumph" has helped you see different ways that you, as a reader, can learn more about the text you are reading. As you continue to work and play with the meaning of texts, you will find that you use some of these angles or lenses more often than others. You may find that one angle is appropriate to a story, and another angle is more useful with an essay.

It is important to know that you do not need to come to a conclusion about the meaning of a work of literature. You may need to form your ideas about the meaning a work has for you at a particular moment. Another day, however, when you are in a different mood or have had an experience that relates to the events described, you may find that your understanding of the story has changed.

Every step you take toward creating richer meaning involves changing perspectives, making connections, and facing new possibilities. You make interpretive decisions each time you look through a different lens. By looking at a work from different angles, you will find your reading becomes more imaginative, intellectual, and emotional.

Collaborating

Read through your logs and think about the various activities you've done with Anne Sexton's poem "To a Friend Whose Work Has Come to Triumph." Talk with your partner about how your understanding or appreciation of the poem has changed or deepened as you have looked at it from different angles, and as you have talked, written, and drawn your ideas.

- What new questions can you ask now?

- Which angles of vision gave you the most insight and the most pleasure as you worked with this poem?

- What else can you say about the meaning of this poem?

Log Entry 7

Using your logs, the text, your own responses, and relevant events in your own experience, write and/or draw your reflections about the meaning of this poem for you now.

Building Your Course Portfolio

Periodically, as you work through this book, we will suggest that you compose a piece for your portfolio. While your writing folder contains notes, first drafts, and short pieces written without extensive revision, your course portfolio is a collection of finished works that represent your best thinking about an idea or works of literature you have been studying. Your portfolio piece may be a piece of writing, a graphic, a live performance, a video presentation, or some combination. For the graphic, video presentation, and oral performance options, which probably will not fit into a portfolio, include a photograph or a carefully written description of your work,

along with notes, scripts, or tapes. In this book we frequently identify possible portfolio pieces as a *portfolio entry*.

Usually the portfolio work will come after you have read a number of related texts. In this introductory section, however, which ac-
quaints you with techniques that you will use throughout the book,
your first portfolio piece will be in response to the poem "To a
Friend Whose Work Has Come to Triumph."

*P*ortfolio Entry

The following is the process for building your portfolio entry:

1. Reread the logs you wrote about the poem for each of the lenses
   or angles of vision.

2. Think about the ideas you would like to work with for your finished work.

3. Once you have decided on an idea that you want to develop, do
   some clustering or brainstorming to generate additional ideas.

As you worked through the various approaches to this one poem,
you enlarged your thinking as you

- recorded your thoughts and feelings.

- looked at parallel stories from your previous reading or experience.

- speculated on how your reading might be different if you had
  changed various aspects of the poem.

- noted how additional information about Sexton affected your
  reading.

- looked at how the form of the poem figured into your understanding.

- recast the poem in different ways.

- reflected on how your understanding or appreciation changed as
  you worked through the various angles of vision.

Content and Form

You will need to consider two aspects of your product: the nature of the *idea* you want to develop and the *form* or *forms* you want to use to develop that idea. Each will affect the other. Following are some options, but don't feel limited by these. You may want to think of your own options.

Written options

- an original poem based on a different myth

- an analysis of the relationship between the original Icarus myth as summarized from Ovid (see p. 74) and the Sexton poem

- a written dialogue based on your logs for Angle 3: Shifting Perspectives

- a short story or personal narrative based loosely on a real-life experience you have had or know about, one that has similarities to the Icarus/Daedalus relationship

- a paper about Anne Sexton and her life, based on additional readings of her poetry

- a paper showing the relationship between a reproduction of Van Gogh's painting "Starry Night" and Sexton's poem. (For this option, you will need to find a reproduction of Van Gogh's painting "Starry Night.")

Graphic options

You probably have the origin of an idea for a graphic in your logs. Look through them for ways you might present your ideas about the work in this chapter.

Graphic options may stand alone, or they may accompany a written option. If the graphic stands alone, you should write a short explanation of your use of symbols, colors, or other means of representation for your portfolio.

For graphics, try to use good quality paper. You will need marking pens, crayons, or watercolors. You do not need to have artistic ability to begin working with graphics; your goal is to translate your ideas into symbols, images, or whatever seems to best represent your visions, using drawings and words as they are appropriate. You are not simply illustrating the work; you are showing how you understand the work.

Here are suggestions that may stimulate some ideas:

- Map the relationship between Icarus and his father. Include in your map similar relationships that you know about from your reading or your experience.

- Design a graphic presenting the story of Icarus as you know it from the poem, from the Greek myth, and from your own related stories.

- Design a graphic presentation that shows your understanding of Sexton's poem "The Starry Night."

Performance options

Performance options may include written work and graphics as well as performances, if they are part of the presentation. You may want to work with a partner or in a small group to prepare a dramatic performance. You may, of course, design a solo presentation. Following are some suggestions:

- Look closely at your log entries for Angle 6: Recasting the Text. Working with a partner, write out and refine one of the suggested dialogues or one of your own. Present your dialogue to a larger group or to the class.

- Look back at the logs you have written for Angles 2, 3, and 6. Working with two or three classmates, prepare a storytelling session, with all of the stories dealing in some way with the relationship between Icarus and Daedalus. Refine your storytelling by listening to each other and making suggestions. Decide which order works best for your stories. Then present your stories to the class.

- Reread "To a Friend Whose Work Has Come to Triumph." With a partner serving as a director, plan the "freeze frames" for significant points in the poem. Plan how you will physically represent Icarus at each point. What facial expressions? What gestures? What stance—standing, kneeling, bending over? Using the director's suggestions, polish your performance for the class. The director will read the poem aloud as you present your interpretation and move from frame to frame.

From Process to Product

The success of your final product—written, graphic, oral, or a combination—depends on your ability to see something through to completion. There are several factors that will help you learn how you work best and how you can take advantage of that knowledge as you develop an idea into its best possible form.

The following steps in working through a major paper or project will help you present your ideas.

1. Messing around

You need to be able to tolerate the "messing around" stage. Often this stage will begin in your journal or log entries. In order to find out exactly what you want to do, however, you need to be able to make a number of starts, often in different directions. You can explore your own best way to get started by trying out different strategies such as clustering, mapping, listing, or brainstorming. (See pages 4–5 for explanations of clustering and mapping.)

2. Making a rough draft, notes, and sketches

Once you have decided on your idea, you need to cultivate your own space in which to write or draw. In your first draft, try to develop your ideas as fully as you can in a short period of time, depending on the scope of your planned work. Once you have your ideas roughly sketched out, you can begin the revising process. Throughout the book, we include ideas to show you how to turn your rough draft into a finished product.

3. Collaborating

We cannot stress enough the value of collaboration once you have a rough draft of your first ideas. This is the time for meeting with response groups to share your work and get feedback from others. Because you are the one who knows what your goal is, you are the one who must tell your responders what you want from them. Sometimes you may just want to have them listen; other times you may want specific revision suggestions. From time to time in this book, we will present specific response-group suggestions and guidelines.

For now, use your best knowledge of what you need from your group, and be sure to give back to the others what they ask of you.

4. Revising

Again, after the collaboration, you will need a quiet time while you further revise and refine. Regardless of the help others may offer, each word or placement of design is ultimately your decision; you will take both the praise and the criticism. This part of the process is often the most satisfying, when you see your work really taking shape and becoming more than you even dreamed of in the beginning.

5. Editing

With written work, this is the final step before publication. At this stage you may need the help of a partner, or you may need to consult a dictionary or writing handbook. If you are using a word processor, be sure to use the spell check, but remember that it does not catch certain kinds of typographical errors (*on* for *one,* for example). You need to proofread carefully and, if possible, get someone else to proofread for you (not because you wouldn't recognize a typo, but because your eyes see what your brain expects.)

6. Publishing

This is the next-to-the-last step. For classroom projects, publication can take many different forms. Finished written projects go into your course portfolio, the collection of work you consider ready for publication. Finished graphics should be accompanied by a presentation to the class and be displayed on the wall of the classroom. Finished performances may be presented to other classes as well as your own. Several of you may plan to take your performance "on the road," presenting it for your school open house, a PTA meeting, or an elementary school assembly. (Our students say that children are often the best audiences.) For finished work that cannot go into the portfolio, write a short, concise explanation of the graphic or oral performance that you did for your project. Include the chapter title, a brief description or title of the assignment that you completed, and a description of the finished work.

7. Evaluating

Although your teacher will be evaluating both your finished product and your work throughout the process, your own evaluation is an important key to your growth as a self-sufficient reader, writer, and performer. It is important to step back and reflect on your accomplishment. Before you can do that usefully, you need to consider what your goals were in the beginning, how they changed as you worked, and how your final product reflects your thinking. Your teacher may provide specific suggestions for self-assessment throughout the chapters. For now, try writing a very short assessment of your final product for this one chapter. In it, state what you hoped to accomplish when you began and how your final work measures up to or exceeds your expectations.

As your portfolio grows, you will be able to trace the record of your best work. At the end of the course, you will have a substantial body of your own work to serve as a record of your growth as a reader, writer, graphic artist, and performer.

2

Transformations:
A Study of Style
and Point of View

*O*riginality is an elusive quality. People crave to be original and at the same time to be like everyone else. Part of each of us wants to be unique, to stand out from the crowd; another part is slave to the fads and fashions of our age, our group, our culture.

*Lo*g Entry 1

Take a few minutes and write about how you see yourself with regard to originality. Include examples of how you are like other people and how you are also original in your thoughts and habits. For example, you might write about how your clothes reflect both your originality and your conventionality. Following are some questions to get you started. Don't try to answer them separately; just use them to jog your thinking.

- How are you most like your friends?

- How are you like other students in your community?

- How are you different from other students in your class?

- How are you different from others in your own circle of friends?

- How do the clothes you are wearing now reflect your originality?

- How do your clothes identify you as a member of a group—an age group, a group of friends, a team, a club?

- Are there clothes in your closet that you wouldn't ever wear again? If so, why have you stopped wearing them? Why haven't you thrown them away?

- On a scale from 1 ("I like to be one of the crowd") to 10 ("I like to think of myself as a complete individualist"), where would you put yourself at this time in your life?

1——2——3——4——5——6——7——8——9——10

- Where do you think other people—a good friend, a parent, a teacher, a coach—would place you? Ask a few of them after you've made a guess. (It might be interesting to make a chart of the results in your log.)

*M*odeling Form and Structure

Writers and artists, like everybody else, crave originality, yet they often want to be like a successful or admired predecessor. You may know that the traditional way artists study painting is to imitate the masters. Many writers, too, either consciously or unconsciously spend their early writing days in a kind of apprenticeship, modeling their work on that of writers they admire. "I once wrote endless imitations," wrote Dylan Thomas, "though I never thought them to be imitations, but, rather, wonderfully original things, like eggs laid by tigers."

Some writers acknowledge that their best work is embedded in the roots of their artistic teachers. Robert Duncan, who influenced many young poets himself, very openly called one of his early books *Derivations* to express his debt to Gertrude Stein, a model not only for Duncan but for Ernest Hemingway and many other writers as well. In a later book, *Roots and Branches,* Duncan also acknowledges the sources of his poetry, the "branches," being "rooted" in the history of the poets he admired from the past. Yet Duncan himself is admired today as one of the most original poets of this century.

Assuming that you want your writing to sound like *you* and not like somebody else, why would you want to spend time modeling the style or form of another writer? One way to begin to understand possible responses to this legitimate question is to try your hand at some specific modeling exercises. In this section, you are asked to try out several different writers' styles by modeling a poem or short passage of prose.

In the exercises that follow, you will be asked to try several ways of organizing your ideas, borrowing the form of the original and changing the outward appearance. The first exercise is an imitation in which you retain some starter words and the form of the original.

Loose Modeling

First read "The Child" by Donald Hall. If possible, have someone read it aloud first; then read it silently to yourself. At this point, just listen for the mood or tone of the poem; don't worry about possible meanings.

The Child

Donald Hall

He lives among a dog,
a tricycle, and a friend.
Nobody owns him.

He walks by himself, beside
the black pool, in the cave
where icicles of rock

rain hard water,
and the walls are rough
with the light of stone.

He hears low talking
without words.
The hand of a wind touches him.

He walks until he is tired
or somebody calls him.
He leaves right away.

When he plays with his friend
he stops suddenly
to hear the black water.

Now select a person to use as the subject for your model of this poem. You might select a person you know well or someone you have observed closely but don't really know. Choose someone whose clothes, habits, or actions you can describe clearly.

Next write a loose model of "The Child" using the form that follows as a guideline (see Figure 2-1). You may write longer or shorter lines, but keep the same number of lines in each stanza and retain the key words as indicated. That's what makes this a "loose model"; you keep a few elements of the original, but change the rest.

Finally, give your poem a title. Titling a poem can be quite difficult, for in a way it demands that we understand what we have created. It's not unusual for a poet to leave a poem untitled, letting the first line serve as identification. Untitled, Hall's poem would be referred to as "He lives among a dog." Before you title your poem, spend time considering and discussing why Hall might have se-

The Child

He lives among a dog,

a tricycle, and a friend.

Nobody owns him.

He walks by himself, beside

the black pool, in the cave

where icicles of rock

rain hard water,

and the walls are rough

with the light of stone.

He hears low talking

without words.

The hand of a wind touches him.

He walks until he is tired

or somebody calls him.

He leaves right away.

When he plays with his friend

he stops suddenly

to hear the black water.

                    Donald Hall

[Right column handwritten entries:] He lives / He walks / He hears / He walks / When

Figure 2-1.

lected the title he did and other possible titles for Hall's poem. Consider following the pattern of "The Child" by using a generic phrase such as "The Mother" or "The Coach" for the title of your poem.

Collaborating

Share your modeled poem with your writing group. Compare notes on how easy or difficult this modeling process was. The important thing to keep in mind about these exercises is that they are just that—exercises. When you are learning a new sport or a new instrument, for example, you spend a lot of time practicing, trying your best but not worrying when things don't go right at first.

If you had trouble modeling this poem, talk with your group about where you got stuck. Maybe someone else had difficulty in the same place. Some students, for example, have trouble modeling stanzas 2 and 3, where the original poem flows from one stanza to another with no punctuation mark. This poetic technique of letting ideas flow from one stanza to the next is called *enjambment*. When you read the example below, notice that the student followed that same pattern. It isn't necessary to follow Hall's punctuation, but some students find it easier to do it that way.

The Sailor
John Goddard

He lives upon the ocean,
the boat, and the churning sea,
lonely day after lonely day.

He walks the weathered deck, along
the violent tide, in his small battered ship
where splinters of rotting wood

fall with each watery knock
and the sails billow softly
with the gust of each new wind.

He hears the whisper of the ocean
in meaningless words
and the cold fingers of the turbulent sea.

He walks in his thoughts along
distantly remembered shores
where life had no problems.

When hours grow long,
he forgets his worries of loneliness
in dreams of someone he left behind.

Work in Progress

There are many poems that can be models for you. We suggest that
you browse through poetry books until you find a poem you like,
then use it as the basis for a poem of your own. Here are two additional poems that you might use as a pattern for a loose model. We
suggest that you read the poem, talk about it with a partner or your
group, and perhaps make a short log entry recording your understanding of the poem. Then turn to the writing of your own poem.
We offer suggestions following each poem, but we also encourage
you to create your own methods for loose modeling.

Swift Things Are Beautiful
Elizabeth Coatsworth

Swift things are beautiful:
Swallows and deer,
And lightning that falls
Bright veined and clear,
Rivers and meteors,
Wind in the wheat,
The strong-withered horse,
The runner's sure feet.

And slow things are beautiful:
The closing of day,
The pause of the wave
That curves downward to spray,
The ember that crumbles,
The opening flower,
And the ox that moves on
In the quiet of power.

Select two antonyms, words that express opposite ideas, such as "swift" and "slow." Following the format loosely, write your own version of "Swift Things Are Beautiful."

Four Little Foxes
Lew Sarett

Speak gently, Spring, and make no sudden sound;
For in my windy valley, yesterday I found
New-born foxes squirming on the ground—
    Speak gently.

Walk softly, March, forbear the bitter blow;
Her feet within a trap, her blood upon the snow,
the four little foxes saw their mother go—
    Walk softly.

Go lightly, Spring, oh, give them no alarm;
When I covered them with boughs to shelter them from harm,
The thin blue foxes suckled at my arm—
    Go lightly.

Step softly, March, with your rampant hurricane;
Nuzzling one another, and whimpering with pain,
The new little foxes are shivering in the rain—
    Step softly.

For this model, select a season. Then decide on a brief phrase directly addressing the season. This kind of direct address to a personified idea is called an *apostrophe,* the same word that we use in making possessives or contractions. Using your apostrophes as a beginning refrain, loosely follow the pattern of "Four Little Foxes," varying the refrain as Sarett does.

Emulation

Next try the style of John Updike, author of many short stories and novels. In this brief excerpt from a story called "Pigeon Feathers," Updike shows a very distinctive sentence pattern, one you will emulate by reproducing the pattern exactly, word for word, using your own ideas and words to replace Updike's. The purpose here is to gain a close understanding of how Updike's sentence patterning supports the meaning he is trying to convey.

Directions for an emulation

1. Replace every word of the original with a word of your own that serves the same grammatical purpose. You don't need to know the parts of speech to do this exercise—we all have a keen ear for sentence structure; but if you do, that means you will replace every noun with a noun, every verb with a verb, every adjective with an adjective, and so on.

2. There are places where you can simply use the words of the original if you want to—words such as *and, but, or* may be kept. Prepositions (words such as *in, out, above, through, with*) may be kept or replaced, and any form of the verb *to be* (*am, is, was, were,* and so on) may be used as in the original.

3. Choose a passage you have already written in your log or write a paragraph or more on a topic that is interesting to you. Shape the passage into Updike's syntax, the sentence pattern, the way each kind of word functions in the sentence. Where Updike has a word with a modifier ("round hole" and "pinched bit"), you have a word with a modifier. Where the Updike passage has an action word ("fly," "fell," "skimming"), so do you.

4. The easiest way to do an emulation is to copy the original on your own paper, typed or handwritten in ink, leaving two spaces after each line. Write your emulation in pencil in the space below the original, keeping your words aligned with those in the original (see Figure 2-2). (These directions might seem like a lot of work for a short exercise, but they will save you time and energy in the long run.)

When you have finished your own emulation, keep writing another sentence or two. Bring your ideas to a natural conclusion while continuing to write in a way that sounds consistent with what you have emulated. The point is to continue to write in the style of the original without the support of its sentence patterns. By taking this extra step, you'll begin to internalize the structure of Updike's sentences.

S h e   s t o o d   t h e r e   i n   t h e   h a l l w a y ,
He lay there on the field,

l e a n i n g   o n   h e r   l o c k e r ,   h e r   h e a d
grimacing from the pain, one leg

b e n t   d o w n   o v e r   a   c r u m p l e d   p i e c e
turned out at an odd sort

o f   p a p e r   i n   h e r   h a n d .
of angle to his body.

Figure 2-2.

Collaborating

Sometimes it is helpful to try out your ideas with a partner while you are doing this exercise. You might also be able to help each other think of appropriate words for difficult spots. If you get completely stuck and neither your teacher nor your partner seems able to help, you may just have to stop and either ask your teacher to help you find another passage to emulate or find one yourself.

Following is a passage from John Updike's "Pigeon Feathers," for your emulation. (Remember to copy this passage, typed or in ink, double spaced.)

It flew in, with a battering of wings, from the outside, and waited there, silhouetted against its pinched bit of sky, preening and cooing in a throbbing, thrilled, tentative way. Neither did it fly. Instead it stuck in the round hole, pirouetting rapidly and nodding its head as if in frantic agreement. Then the pigeon fell into a handful of rags, skimming down the barn wall into the layer of straw that coated the floor of the mow on this side.

Following is an example of an emulation written to the John Updike passage by David Suico when he was a student. Notice that he has added one long sentence of his own to the emulation, finishing his idea and retaining the rhythm of the Updike passage.

It crept in, with a blowing of steam, from the pass, and stopped there, surrounded by its strange kind of home, hissing and clanging in a pulsating, chilled, rhythmic manner. Neither did it stop. Instead, it stood on the hardened steel, vibrating constantly and generating its power as if in harmonic motion. Then the train moved out of a station of people, edging down the wooden platform into the openness of the valley that filled the landscape of the bottom of this mountain range. Slowly gaining speed, stopping not for anyone or anything, the train rambled across the wooden trestle bridge that spanned the mighty river, through the open pastures and the dense forest of oak, finally coming to a rest in the city at the heart of the valley.

Look for the point when the emulation stopped and David's addition began. If he was successful, you had to look at the original Updike passage to determine where the break falls. Test your own extensions with your group.

What can be interesting, even fascinating, about this kind of writing is that it yields rich new meanings. In fact, the need to create meaning rather than nonsense is, according to most students, irresistible. Consider your own struggle with this challenging assignment. It would have been nearly effortless to throw words down on a page—to dash off the required number of lines with no thought at all. But the chances are that you didn't do that; you struggled with your words and your lines. Yet nowhere were you directly asked to create a coherent meaningful version of the original. Discuss what seems to be a human need to make meaning.

You might also discuss the related question of ownership. Whose words are these anyhow? Whose meaning, yours or the author of the original?

Log Entry 2

1. Write a page or so in your log expressing your ideas about this exercise. How do you feel about the results of your emulation?

2. Speculate in your log about the matters you discussed with your group—the subject of the human need to make meaning and the question of ownership.

Spin-off or Response Modeling

In spin-off or response modeling, you respond directly to the meaning and tone of the original, but you do not model the form.

First read the following poem.

Poem to be Read at 3:00 A.M.
Donald Justice

Excepting the diner
On the outskirts,
The town of Ladora
At 3 A.M.
Was dark but
For my headlights
And up in
One second-story room
A single light
Where someone
Was sick or
Perhaps reading
As I drove past
At seventy
Not thinking
This poem
Is for whoever
Had the light on.

Collaborating

With a partner or your group, study Donald Justice's poem again. Notice that although it isn't punctuated, it is composed of just two sentences, one relatively long (forty-four words), the other short (nine words). What would happen to the poem if a period were inserted in an appropriate place? Where is an appropriate place? What does this suggest to you about poetry, punctuation, or writing in general?

Also consider and discuss why the poet must have chosen not to punctuate and why he made the first sentence so long as compared to the second sentence. What might the punctuation have to do with the meaning of the poem?

Work in Progress

Read through all of the following options for spin-off modeling before you select which of them you want to do. If you come up with a better idea, use it for a spin-off poem. Put your draft into your writing folder.

- Pretend you were the person who was in the room with the light on at 3:00 A.M. Think of some reasons why you might have been up at three in the morning. Write a poem as if you were speaking to the driver.

- Be someone in the house, but focus on the driver in your poem. Why would someone be driving through town at that hour? Was that person male or female? Alone or with someone? Why were they driving so fast? Write your response in the form of a poem.

Log Entry 3

Look at the poem or poems you wrote in response to Justice's poem. How did you decide where to put the punctuation or whether to use any at all? What does the punctuation of your poem have to do with its meaning? Write down some of your ideas about Justice's poem, your poem, or the whole question of punctuation and meaning.

Here is one student's recasting of the Donald Justice poem:

Poem to be Read after Reading "Poem to be Read at 3:00 A.M."
Reggie Bailey

It's 3 A.M. and I just had a fight with my parents.
Everybody has gone to bed.
They were mad because they said I was home late
And again they accused me of smoking dope.
I don't think I can take any more of this.
I want to split now,
But something keeps holding me back.
I lie on my bed
Thinking
What I should do.
After awhile I get up and go to the window.
I see a Volkswagen speeding past my house.
I wonder to myself who is in the car
And why it is going through town at this time
And so fast.
I wonder if maybe the driver is running from something
Or if there is an emergency.
I turn off the light
And go to bed
Thinking
About the car and the driver.

Idea Modeling

Sometimes reading just a title or a line will be enough to trigger an idea for your own writing. In idea modeling, there is no need to retain the original writer's form or tone. Instead of responding directly to the author, as you did in spin-off modeling, you are simply using the author's ideas to trigger your own.

The next few exercises are structured to lead you from an idea in the original poem to a poem of your own. Although the suggestions are quite specific, they are intended only as guidelines. You may choose to expand on one suggestion and bypass another. The important thing is to follow your own inclinations—once you sense what they are. These exercises contain ideas to help you explore possibilities.

Variations on a plum

This poem by William Carlos Williams has been modeled frequently by writers. The story goes that the poem was found on the refrigerator by the poet's wife. If you would like to know more about this poet, a second poem by Williams can be found on page 75 and stories about this poet and physician appear on pages 94 and 117.

This Is Just to Say
William Carlos Williams

I have eaten
the plums
that were in
the icebox

and which
you were probably
saving
for breakfast.

Forgive me
they were delicious
so sweet
and so cold.

*Lo*g Entry 4

This poem has inspired many other poets and students to write "This Is Just to Say" poems. Brainstorm a list of other situations that would require a note such as this poem.

Following are two models by high school students. As you read them, think about variations you might want to try.

This Is Just to Say

Cal Coolidge

I have left you
some candy
which you'll find on the counter,

and which
you are probably avoiding
on your diet.

Forgive me.
You are so careful,
so healthy,
and so annoying.

Variations on Cal's Variations on Williams

Judd Piggott

I have copied
the poem
that Cal was writing,

and which he was probably using
for credit.

Forgive me,
it was so fitting,
so good,
and so easy.

*W*ork in Progress

Try your own versions of "This Is Just to Say." Write several and leave them around—on the refrigerator, lockers, mirrors—anywhere. Keep in mind that when you do, your poem will be just as "published" as Williams's was when he first pasted "This Is Just to Say" on his own refrigerator door.

Variations on a line or title

Sometimes just the first line of a poem will give you an idea for a poem. "Interior Decoration" begins with that kind of provocative line.

Interior Decoration
Adrien Stoutenburg

I am thinking of doing over my room,
of plastering wings on it,
of letting clouds in through the attic,
of collecting moles
and training them to assemble in an oval
for a rug as bright as black water:
of growing orchids under the couch
    for a lavender surprise
    against the sleeping dust;
of inviting wind to the closet—
    empty shapes will blow and sing like sails—
of planting a quail's nest in a yellow corner—
    eggs in time will hatch out stumbling flowers—
of taking a fox for a companion—
    his fur will be my fire on cold days—
of building a great square silo of books:
    pale green, blue (moss color, sky color),
     deep red, russet, orange (sun and blowing leaf color)
    their spines scrawled with loud gold
    and chiming silver—ARABIA DESERTA,
    LETTERS OF RILKE, WALDEN,
    HUNGER, BEYOND GOOD AND EVIL.
These, when the blizzard comes,
will be my soaring walls.

*Lo*g Entry 5

Try the following sequence:

1. Most people think of interior decorators as people who plan other people's living spaces—selecting color schemes, choosing furnishings, rugs, even posters and paintings. Here,

however, the word *interior* seems to have another meaning. Take a few minutes to record in your log any lines that appeal to you and your reasons for recording them. Then jot down some ideas of things you would bring into your dream room—things that would be your "soaring walls" "when the blizzard comes."

2. Draw or sketch the floor plan of the space you consider yours. It might be your bedroom, or the part of the room you share with someone else; it might be a practice room, if you are a musician. It might even be some space you have carved out for yourself where you are completely responsible for what goes into the area and how it is arranged. On the floor plan, indicate what is now in this space. You can indicate a chair by sketching in a simple square and labeling it, or you can actually draw it in.

3. Imagine that you have just the same space you have now, but you can transform it any way you choose. Draw another floor plan, and this time decorate it as you would if you could translate your dream space into reality. There is no limit here other than the actual space with its windows, doors, and dimensions. You might want to reread the poem to get a sense of fantasy, but you have the choice of making your room either realistic or dreamlike.

Work in Progress

Using your ideas or drawings as a guide, write your own poem beginning "I am thinking of doing over . . . "

Scar trek

The next exercise has to do with scars (the heading for this section is not a typographical error). Before reading the following poems that explore the idea of how some people feel about their scars, take a few minutes to write in your log.

*L*og Entry 6

Cluster or jot down all of the associations you have with the word *scar*. If you come to an association that you don't want to explore, bypass it and go on. Work quickly to get details down in a word or two—just enough so that you can recall what you meant.

You might begin with physical scars, recording such data as

* your age when the incident happened.

* the other people who were involved.

* where the incident happened (include details, if you can).

* anything else that is relevant.

When you have dealt with your physical scars, you might go on to cluster the ones that leave no marks on the body—emotional scars, scars on the land, or any other associations you have with the word *scar*. Now read William Dickey's poem.

Memoranda

William Dickey

The scars take us back to places we have been,
Cities named Masochism or Inaccuracy.
This little one between the finger and the thumb
Is something that my brother did to me
On a hot Washington's Birthday in the past,
When we were young and cruelly competent;
In a miniature world like a glass fishing float
He was the total image of intent.

Who stuck the pencil point into my palm?
It was so long ago that I cannot say;
But the black stick of graphite under the skin—
Some friend, some enemy put it there that way
to succeed in calling himself always to mind.
Action has consequence, and though his face
Has faded into the city of the lost,
I look at my hand and see the injured place.

Like hasty marks on an explorer's chart:
This white stream bed, this blue lake on my knee
Are an angry doctor at midnight, or a girl
Looking at the blood and trying not to see
What we both have seen. Most of my body lives,
But the scars are dead like the grooving of a frown,
Cannot be changed, and ceaselessly record
How much of me is already written down.

Vincent Wixon provides another angle on scars in "Looking at My Hands." Like William Dickey, Vincent Wixon is a teacher as well as a poet.

Looking at My Hands

Vincent Wixon

Back of my right hand rises a white scar—
spike wound from wrestling in the outfield.
I read that the guy's plane
went down in Vietnam.

People have said I have good hands;
I catch footballs, baseballs easily.
Why, then, is my handwriting so lousy?
Why don't I juggle?
Then there's the scar on my left first finger
from cutting backwards with a jack knife.
The den mother warned us.

I used to be vain about them—
long strong fingers, slender palms.
Now the skin looks old,
veins blue and prominent;
psoriasis eats the nails warping like old paper.

Collaborating

William Dickey writes in his poem that "scars take us back to places we have been"; he might have added, to the "person" we have been. In your writing group, discuss the incidents that Dickey and Wixon relate in their poems and how they have turned them into poems. Then talk with each other about accidents that have resulted in scars that you carry, scars that take you back or, perhaps, forward. Your group may choose to discuss environmental and emotional scars, but stay with your own experiences and share only those scars you feel comfortable talking about.

*W*ork in Progress

Choose a focus for a poem or prose piece of your own in which you explore some aspect of scars. You might choose a physical scar and write a short account of the accident that caused it. You might, as William Dickey and Vincent Wixon did, write about several scars, drawing some generalization from the cluster; or you may choose to write about an emotional scar. If you write about scars on the land, environmental scars, try to personalize the topic so that your reader will know how the land scar affects you personally, not just people in the abstract sense. None of these suggested approaches to the general subject of scars exhausts the possibilities, of course, so feel free to move out beyond them.

The following poem, written by a high school junior and titled simply "Scars," was the first poem that Margaret Mullens ever wrote. Do you agree that it shows how the power of a recreated memory can take over one's writing? Discuss how. Also consider after a first reading how the meaning of this particular poem may be intensified by being read aloud.

Scars

Margaret Mullens

This gloomy day brings memories of scars,
scars of my memories.
The day which almost ended my life,
the doctor left his mark.
The stitch lines

bring back that rainy day
my mother's face in horror
at my screams.
The red lights
flashing through my mind.
The white stretcher,
white uniforms, tubes in my arms.
I remember no more,
but the scar
mars my stomach.
The physical scars of my life
are healed
to be laughed about
or to have something
for conversation.
Can I speak of my emotional scars?
Can I face them?
Can I heal them?
If I could see my heart, I know the
scars would be deep,
ugly, protruding, showing,
condemning me.
My family, my friends.
The beat gets louder
and louder
the scars open and close,
open and close.
They scream for
medicine.
They bleed for
healing.
The infection
grows,
overcomes me.
I think,
weep
for these hidden scars.

This next poem's title is a play on words, much as in Stouten-burg's "Interior Decoration." In this poem, student Melanie Anne Gauché recounts a familiar experience.

States of Mind
Melanie Anne Gauché

I. Rhode Island
White snow, blinding snow;
Kids laughing and playing.
Sledding faster, faster;
Tree, Crash, Blood.
Brave girl, lucky girl,
Twelve stitches on top of her head.

II. Florida
Big fights, frantic fights. Kids crying and wondering.
Could it be us, was it us?
Arguing, yelling, slam!
It's OK Mom. It's OK Dad.
But it wasn't.

III. California
Loud mother-child quarrels.
"Why does she do this to me?"
"I hate her!"
Accusations, threats, smack!
It's not OK, but I'm fine.
Dad and I both are, here.

The next student poem was much longer in its first draft. Jana Hunt and her writing group worked to see how she could make the poem more concise while retaining the essence of the childhood experience that resulted in her scars.

Right Now They're Invisible
Jana Hunt

White hidden in whiteness,
like the famous picture of the white cow
eating marshmallows in a snow storm
that children talk about,
but when summer comes
and my skin begins to tan,
they will appear like secret messages
written in invisible ink by a Russian spy.

When I look at these three white blotches
shaped like the Great Lakes on my elbow,
I see myself standing
on tip-toe
struggling to reach the counter-top
that was then six inches
above my head.

I see my fingers
grasping for the cookies
placed purposely beyond my reach,
and instead catching hold of the cord,
and screaming as coffee grounds
and black pools of water splattered
and splashed, and my mother,
her make-up half on and her hair
in rollers, running in and
"Why can't you be more careful?
. . . like a bull in a china shop. . . ."
Then she saw I was crying, and the blood,
and held my elbow under the faucet
letting the cool water wash over it,
apologizing over and over, and I cried
as I watched the red skin blister,
not knowing that the sun
would one day make me remember
how it felt to be small.

Beyond Modeling: The Paralogue

The last exercise we will suggest in this section involves a rather different kind of thinking. In the *paralogue,* you actually enter into a kind of dialogue with the author. The prefix *para-* means "alongside" or "by the side of," and the word root *log* or *logue* means "written or spoken language." So a *paralogue* refers to a piece of writing in which a reader responds directly to the author, either line by line or section by section. The result is a piece of writing in two voices, the original author's and the respondent's.

*P*ortfolio Entry

1. Set up a page as you do for your double-entry log. You will use this format for a rough draft of your paralogue.

2. For this exercise, you will read a short prose excerpt entitled "Search for the Heron" from *River Notes* by Barry Lopez. Read just the first paragraph. Don't worry if you don't know all the words or if it doesn't make a lot a sense to you at this point. This passage may seem mysterious; you may not even know what Lopez is writing about, but that is okay. Writing the paralogue will let you see that you often can understand the tone or feeling of a piece even when you are not sure of its meaning.

   > I see you on the far side of the river, standing at the edge of familiar shadows, before a terrified chorus of young alders on the bank. I do not think you know it is raining. You are oblivious to the "thuck" of drops rolling off the tube of your neck and the slope of your back. Above, in the sweepy cedars, drops pool at the tips of leather needles, break away, are sheered by the breeze and, "thuck," hit the hollow-boned, crimson-colored shoulders of the bird and fall swooning into the river.

3. To begin the rough draft of your paralogue, select one sentence from the passage you have just read (it isn't necessary to account for your choice), or you may use phrases from different parts of the passage and make them into a sentence. Write this sentence or the sentence parts on the left side of your log, the original author's side. (Examples begin on page 49.)

4. Now on the right side of the log, your side, write a sentence of your own in response to the sentence you wrote on the left. When you have written your sentence, read this next passage from Barry Lopez:

   > Perhaps you know it is raining. The intensity of your stare is then not oblivion, only an effort to spot between the rain splashes in the river (past your feet, so well-known, there beneath the hammered surface like twigs in the pebbles) the movement of trout.

5. Follow the same procedure that you did previously. Select a sentence from Lopez, answer it with a sentence of your own, then go on to read the next passage:

I know: your way is to be inscrutable. When pressed, you leave. This is no more unexpected or mysterious than that you give birth to shadows. Or silence. I watch from a distance. With respect. I think of standing beside you when you have died of your own brooding over the water—as shaken as I would be at the collapse of a cathedral, wincing deep inside as at the screech of an overloaded cart.

6. Continue the same pattern: select a sentence from Lopez, copy it in column one of your log, and write your response in column two. Then read the following passage:

You carry attribution well, refusing to speak. With your warrior's feathers downsloped at the back of your head, those white sheaves formed like a shield overlaying your breast, your gray-blue cast, the dark tail feathers—do you wear wolves' tails about your ankles and dance in clearings in the woods when your blood is running? I wonder where you have fought, warrior. Where!

7. Again, select a sentence from Lopez and write a responding one. Then read the last passage:

You retreat beneath your cowl, spread wings, rise, drift upriver as silent as winter trees. I follow you. You have caught me with your reticence. I will listen to whatever they say about you, what anyone who has seen you wishes to offer—and I will return to call across the river to you, to confirm or deny. If you will not speak, I will have to consider making you up.

8. Finish the rough draft of your paralogue by selecting a sentence or combining phrases to make a sentence from Lopez's words and writing it in column one. Then write your concluding sentence in column two.

   To turn your rough draft into a finished paralogue, read your rough draft as a whole, from left to right, sentence by sentence. First read Lopez's words, then your own, as you would a dialogue. At this point, make any changes you want. You may go back and add or subtract words from Lopez's side, but don't use any words or phrases here that are not part of the original. On your side, change anything you would like to make your words read more smoothly. You will probably be surprised at how much like a dialogue your draft sounds. When you're satisfied with the words, give your paralogue a title and make a final copy of it, using the following pattern:

	Title
WORDS FROM LOPEZ	YOUR WORDS
Lopez	
	You
Lopez	
	You

Collaborating

Your last step before publishing is, of course, to read your paralogue aloud with a partner. Have your partner read Lopez's words; you read your words. Then do the same for your partner's paralogue. Once you have read your work through a couple of times, you might want to share your paralogue aloud with the class.

Following are three examples of paralogues. The first two were written by students; the third was written by a teacher.

Paralogue
Julie Chatt

LOPEZ   ME
I see you on the far side of the
river, standing at the edge of
familiar shadows. I do not
think you know it is raining; you
are oblivious to the "thuck" of drops.

                                I see you so far away from me, yet I
                                see where I once was so close. You do
                                not know that I am here. You are
                                oblivious to my presence.
The intensity of your stare is then
not oblivion, only an effort
to spot between the rain splashes
in the river.

                                I can see what you are thinking. You
                                are searching my face to see if
                                what I say is true.

LOPEZ   ME

When pressed, you leave. This
is no more unexpected than that you
give birth to shadows. I watch from
a distance. I think of standing
beside you when you have died, as
shaken as I would be at the collapse
of a cathedral.

                              You are afraid of lies so you retreat
                              as always. I watch you. I think
                              of how crushed I would be if
                              you ever left me.

Your feathers downsloped at the
back of your head, the white
sheaves formed like a shield
overlaying your breast. I
wonder where you have fought.

                              Your eyes are clouded, acting as
                              a shield to hide your heart. I
                              wonder who or what has hurt
                              you so deeply to create this
                              strong outer shield you possess.

You retreat beneath your cowl.
I follow you. You have caught
me with your reticence.

                              You run away from me to your own
                              little world. I follow you as
                              far as I can go. You entice
                              me with your innocence. You
                              are so frightened. I will not hurt you.

Brave Young

Tricia Lehmkuhl

LOPEZ   ME

You are oblivious to the "thuck"
of drops rolling off the tube of your
neck and the slope of your back.

                              I see only you, your face, your
                              hands. The rain seems an invisible
                              curtain which must be parted
                              if I am to touch you.

Perhaps you know it is raining.
The intensity of your stare is
then not oblivion . . .

LOPEZ   ME

                                   I feel the rain, the cool droplets
                                   of Mothers Earth's tears. My
                                   stare is not into oblivion, but
                                   into two pools of blue crystal,
                                   falls my heart to you.

When pressed, you leave. This
is no more unexpected or
mysterious than that
you give birth to shadows.
Or silence. I watch from a distance.

                                   I have been summoned. I must go.
                                   We have expected this a long while
                                   and should I not come home,
                                   remember me. The shadow falls
                                   upon my face as I am pulled from the
                                   river. You watch from a distance.

You carry attribution well,
refusing to speak. I wonder where
you have fought, warrior.

                                   I speak a language you know
                                   not. I have fought in lands
                                   you could not imagine. Yes,
                                   I am a warrior, fighting for
                                   you.

I follow you. You have caught
me with your reticence.

                                   I see you through the shadows,
                                   your face, your hands. It seems
                                   you are following me. Why?
                                   I know not where I am to go—
                                   to heaven? To hell? Will I be
                                   with you?

I watch from a distance.
With respect. I think of standing
beside you unless you have died.

                                   Still in the shadow (of what is this
                                   shadow caused?) I watch the crystal
                                   pools come closer. It is hot, hard to
                                   breathe. Tears run from my eyes as
                                   you move closer. Blackness over-
                                   takes my eyes, and I finally feel your
                                   touch. The shadow is gone, we are
                                   warm. No longer do I watch you from
                                   a distance, no longer do I fight, no
                                   longer do we not speak one language,
                                   no longer am I a warrior.

Paralogue with Barry Lopez
Markie Short

LOPEZ   ME

I see you on the far side of the river,
standing at the edge of familiar shadows,
before a terrified chorus of young alders
on the bank.

                          First day of school. Teacher, you spend
                          time explaining, demonstrating, chalking
                          up the board, and we are nervous,
                          wondering if we can survive you.

The intensity of your stare is then
not oblivion.

                          Teacher, did we lose you? I think
                          your dreaming has taken you out of
                          this room.

I think of standing beside you when
you have died of your own brooding
over the water.

                          Teacher, don't take our attitude
                          personally. It's not your fault that
                          we don't care.

With your warrior's feathers downsloped
at the back of your head . . .

                          Teacher, you're back again and armed
                          with enthusiasm, concern, and hope.
                          You're getting hard to ignore.

You retreat beneath your cowl, spread
wings, rise, drift upriver as silent
as winter trees.

                          You watch us as we write, you read
                          over our shoulders, you raise your
                          eyebrows; sometimes you smile or nod.
                          We are sweating.

I follow you.

                          We are trying to follow you.

Reflecting on the Modeling Process

Think about what you have learned about how you work, how you
think, and, of course, how you read and write. Modeling is a
process that requires close reading, often with careful attention to
the way words are put together; this is one way of looking at a

writer's style. Generating poems or prose passages that create the same tone and feeling in your own words helps you understand tone and feeling.

Modeling allows you to try out different authors' ways of forming ideas. Modeling allows you to begin to see how structure and style are directly tied to an author's ideas. You won't develop your own style in writing by modeling, but you can begin to explore what different styles feel like, and which ones come closest to how you like to express yourself. Style in writing, as in dress, evolves as we develop our entire personalities. "Our habits make our style," said poet and teacher Josephine Miles. Modeling involves a writer in conscious shaping of structure and language. Use it when you are intrigued by a piece of writing and want to understand it better.

Changing Point of View

One of the things that writers can do at will is adopt a mask or facade, a *persona*, to change who they are as they speak. A writer can take on the persona of anybody, in any place, in any time. Or a writer can take the persona of an animal, or through the power of language, try to give voice to the animal that the writer imagines. To create a persona requires that you use your mind to create the thoughts of another, to imagine how another might think. Always behind the created persona, however, is the sense of its creator, the imagining mind that has taken on the vision of another.

An effective writer draws the reader into the point of view of the persona who is telling the story or describing a scene. The words remain words, however, until an active reader enters into that point of view. You will never know whether the eyes you look through as a reader are the same as those of the persona the writer has assumed, but that doesn't really matter. What matters is the exchange of vision that happens when the reader transforms the words on the page into images, actions, and ideas.

Earlier in this chapter, you practiced taking on other writers' structural forms. They provided the skeleton, and you provided the flesh and blood. To work with other forms in that way helped hone your proficiency as an active reader as well as augment your options as a more informed writer. In this section, you are going to be both active reader and adaptable writer. You will read a number of poems in which writers have adopted personas or in some way have attempted to probe the consciousness of an animal or object. Then you'll do much the same thing—you'll try to get inside the different personas that you choose. You will try to adopt that double vision of the writer that allows you to retain your own knowledge while looking out from other eyes.

Log Entry 7

Think about what it means to assume the consciousness of an animal, as some poets have. Jot down some notes in your log about the following ideas:

- What animal has always interested you or drawn your attention?

- What animal are you most like?

- What relationship can you see between the animal that most interests you and the one you think you are most like? Or are they the same?

- Of the animals you have been thinking about, which do you think you understand the best? This may be your choice for an exercise on changing your point of view later in this section. You don't have to decide just yet, however. Wait until you have had a chance to read some poems in which writers have adopted the persona of an animal.

Collaborating

With your partner or a group, discuss any experiences you may have had with a hawk or other large bird. Following are some suggestions for starters. Use only those that activate your own knowledge or memory.

- How can you tell a hawk from an eagle? From a buzzard? What feelings do these birds evoke? How do you account for any differences in your reaction to these birds?

- Why do most people admire the hawk, which is a predator, and disdain the buzzard, which feeds only on carrion (dead animals)?

- If you have ever seen a hawk make a kill, describe it.

- Have you ever killed a wild bird or a wild animal of any kind? Even with a car? Briefly describe that experience.

Developing Points of View

The reason for thinking about these questions before you read the two poems that follow is to establish a mindset for your reading. The poem that you are going to read first, "Hurt Hawks" by Robinson Jeffers, will have a different meaning for each of you as readers, depending on the experiences you have had with hawks, the feeling you have about killing an animal, and even the attitude you have toward poetry itself. Add to these factors all that Robinson Jeffers brings to the poem—his own passions about animals, his intense feeling for the craggy cliffs where he lived, and his belief in the power of language to convey both feeling and conviction. Out of the interplay between your experiences and the poet's words will emerge the meaning of this poem for you.

Robinson Jeffers lived in a stone house he built himself on a cliff above the rugged Pacific coast. It's easy to imagine this man, who wrote looking out from his "Hawk Tower," actually experiencing the occasion that the "I" of the poem records in "Hurt Hawks," but as readers, we shouldn't make that assumption. As you read this poem, put yourself in the place of the speaker, the "I." As always with poetry, it's best if you can first listen to the poem being read aloud.

Hurt Hawks
Robinson Jeffers

The broken pillar of the wing jags from the clotted shoulder,
The wing trails like a banner in defeat,
No more to use the sky forever but live with famine
And pain a few days: cat nor coyote
Will shorten the week of waiting for death, there is game without
    talons.

He stands under the oak-bush and waits
The lame feet of salvation; at night he remembers freedom
And flies in a dream, the dawns ruin it.
He is strong and pain is worse to the strong, incapacity is worse.
The curs of the day come and torment him
At distance, no one but death the redeemer will humble that head,
The intrepid readiness, the terrible eyes.
The wild god of the world is sometimes merciful to those
That ask mercy, not often to the arrogant.
You do not know him, you communal people, or you have forgotten
    him;
Intemperate and savage, the hawk remembers him;
Beautiful and wild, the hawks, and men that are dying, remember
    him.

I'd sooner, except the penalties, kill a man than a hawk; but the
    great redtail
Had nothing left but unable misery
From the bone too shattered for mending, the wing that trailed
    under his talons when he moved.
We had fed him six weeks, I gave him freedom,
He wandered over the foreland hill and returned in the evening,
    asking for death,
Not like a beggar, still eyed with the old
Implacable arrogance. I gave him the lead gift in the twilight.
    What fell was relaxed,
Owl-downy, soft feminine feathers; but what
Soared: the fierce rush: the night-herons by the flooded river
    cried fear at its rising
Before it was quite unsheathed from reality.

*L*og Entry 8

By talking with your discussion group and then writing in your log,
work through your responses to this poem. If you need a starting
point, try: How did you feel at the end? Then attempt to figure out
what made you feel that way, using both the poem and your own
experiences to reach your understanding of the poem.

Because our focus in this section is point of view, try to get inside the mind of the speaker of this poem. We don't, of course, know whether this is Jeffers himself speaking; he may have adopted another persona in this poem although it could be Jeffers. Work through the idea of whose mind is at work.

- How does Jeffers take you inside the consciousness of the hawk? Do you get a sense of knowing how much of the "hawk-consciousness" is really that of the hawk and how much is the mind of the poet?

- When Jeffers says the hawk is "asking for death," do you believe that it's Jeffers speaking or the consciousness of the hawk?

- Why do you think Jeffers titled this poem "Hurt Hawks" rather than "Hurt Hawk"? How does the plural color the poem's meaning?

Now listen to "Hawk Roosting" by Ted Hughes. Your teacher or a student might read it to the whole class before you read it silently to yourself. Then, again in groups, work through some of the ideas about whose consciousness this is.

Hawk Roosting
Ted Hughes

I sit in the top of the wood, my eyes closed.
Inaction, no falsifying dream
Between my hooded head and hooked feet:
Or in sleep rehearse perfect kills and eat.

The convenience of the high trees!
The air's buoyancy and the sun's ray
Are of advantage to me;
And the earth's face upward for my inspection.

My feet are locked upon the rough bark.
It took the whole of Creation
To produce my foot, my each feather:
Now I hold creation in my foot

Or fly up, and revolve it all slowly—
I kill where I please because it is all mine.
There is no sophistry in my body:
My manners are tearing off heads—

The allotment of death.
For the one path of my flight is direct
Through the bones of the living.
No arguments assert my right:

The sun is behind me.
Nothing has changed since I began.
My eye has permitted no change.
I am going to keep things like this.

Log Entry 9

In "Hawk Roosting," the listener/reader is in the mind of the hawk, looking out from behind those eyes.

Jot down the answers to the following questions:

- For those of you who know hawks from your own observations, how accurate is Hughes's portrayal of the hawk?

- Whose consciousness is in such lines as "Now I hold creation in my foot"? What does that line mean to you?

Collaborating

With a partner or a small group, reread these two poems from the standpoint of whose awareness, whose mind dominates the poem. Read them just to get a sense of how the balance shifts when the writer attempts to get inside the mind of an animal. We can never really do that, of course, any more than we can ever really get inside the mind of another person, except one we make up for a story.

In what ways does the attempt to portray the inside view of the animal reveal the mind of the writer?

After discussing these two poems, talk about how you created your own versions of them, depending on your personal experiences with birds or hawks and with poetry. Share which poem you found more revealing about the nature of hawks and which was more in keeping with your beliefs about wild animals or birds particularly.

Seeing Through Other Eyes

"The Cow's Death," a story by the Irish writer Liam O'Flaherty, comes very close to taking us inside the consciousness of the cow even though O'Flaherty stays with third-person point of view throughout. Read the story and test out your own sense of this cow's reactions to the loss of her calf. Remember that the meaning of this story, as of everything you read, is going to be built on what you bring to the reading as well as what the author actually writes. You may have had no experience at all with cows, but you can draw on your own experience with the feelings that parents have for their children to comprehend the cow's distress.

The Cow's Death
Liam O'Flaherty

The calf was stillborn. It came from the womb tail first. When its red, unwieldy body dropped on the greensward it was dead. It lay with its head doubled about its neck in a clammy mass. The men stood about it and shook their heads in silence. The wife of the peasant who owned the cow sighed and said, "It is God's will." The cow moaned, mad with the pain of birth. Then she wheeled around cumbersomely, her hoofs driving into the soft earth beneath the weight of her body. She stooped over the calf and moaned, again smelling it. Then she licked the still body with her coarse tongue lovingly. The woman rubbed the cow's matted forehead, and there was a tear in her eye; for she too was a mother.

Then the cow, overcome once more with the pain, moved away from the calf and stood with her head bent low, breathing heavily through her nostrils. The breath came in long pale columns, like sunbeams coming through the window of a darkened church. They drove her away to a corner of the field, and she stood wearily with her head over the fence, lashing her flanks with her tail restlessly.

They seized the calf and dragged it by the feet along the field to the fence, out through the fence into another field, then through another fence, then up the grassy slope that led to the edge of the cliff. They dropped it downwards into the sea. It lay in a pulped mass on the rocks. They rebuilt the gaps in the stone fences carefully and returned to the cow. The woman offered her a hot drink of oatmeal, but she refused it. They seized her and poured the drink down her throat, using a bull's horn as a funnel. The cow half swallowed the drink, half tossed it away with her champing mouth.

Then they went home, the woman still moaning the dead calf and apologizing to God for her sorrow. The peasant remained with the cow, watching until she should drop the bag. He buried it under a mound of stones. He dug his heel in the ground, and, taking a handful of the brown earth, he made the sign of the cross on the cow's side. Then he too went home.

For a long time the cow stood leaning over the fence, until the pain lessened. She turned around suddenly and lowed and tossed her head. She took a short run forward, the muscles of her legs creaking like new boots. She stopped again, seeing nothing about her in the field. Then she began to run around by the fence, putting her head over it here and there, lowing. She found nothing. Nothing answered her call. She became wilder as the sense of her loss became clearer to her consciousness. Her eyes became red around the rims and fierce like a bull's. She began to smell around on the ground, half running, half walking, stumbling clumsily among the tummocks of grass.

There was where she had lain in travail, on the side of a little slope, the grass compressed and faded by the weight of her body. There was where she had given birth, the ground trampled by many feet and torn here and there, with the brown earth showing though. Then she smelt where the calf had lain. There were wet stains on the grass. She looked around her fiercely, and then she put her nose to the ground and started to follow the trail where they had dragged the calf to the fence. At the fence she stopped and smelt a long time, wondering with her stupid brain whither the trail led. And then stupidly she pressed with her great bulk against the fence. The stones cut her breast, but she pressed harder in terror and the fence fell before her. She stumbled through the gap and cut her left thigh near the udder. She did not heed the pain, but pressed forward, smelling the trail and snorting.

Faster she went, and now and again she raised her head and lowed—a long, mournful low that ended in a fierce crescendo, like the squall of wind coming around a corner. At the second fence she pushed again. Again she pressed against it, and again it fell before her. Going through the gap she got caught, and in the struggle to get through she cut both her sides along the flanks. The blood trickled through jaggedly, discoloring the white streak on the left flank. She came at a run up the grassy slope to the cliff. She shuddered and jerked aside when she suddenly saw the sea and heard it rumbling distantly below—the waves seething on the rocks and the sea birds calling dismally with their noisome cackle. She smelt the air in wonder. Then she slowly advanced, inch by inch, trembling. When she reached the summit, where the grass ended in a gravel belt that dropped down to the sheer slope of rock, she rushed backwards and circled around wildly, lowing. Again she came up, and planting her feet carefully on the gravel, she looked down. The trail of her calf ended there. She could follow it no further. It was lost in the emptiness beyond that gravel ledge. She tried to smell the air, but nothing reached her nostrils but the salt smell of the sea. She moaned and her sides heaved with the outrush of her breath. Then she looked down, straining out her neck. She saw the body of her calf on the rocks below. She uttered a joyful cry and ran backwards, seeking a path to descend. Up and down the summit of the cliff she went, smelling here and there, looking out over the edge, going on her knees and looking down and finding nowhere a path that led to the object on the rocks below. She came back again, her hind legs clashing as she ran, to the point where the body had been dropped over the precipice.

She strained out and tapped with her fore hoof, scratching the gravel and trying to descend, but there was nothing upon which she could place her feet—just a sheer drop of one hundred feet of cliff and her calf lay on the rocks below.

She stood stupidly looking at it a long time, without moving a muscle. Then she lowed, calling to her calf, but no answer came. She saw the water coming in with the tide, circling around the calf on the rocks. She lowed again, warning it. Wave after wave came in, eddying around the body. She lowed again and tossed her head wildly as if she wanted to buffet the waves with her horns.

And then a great wave came towering in, and catching up the calf on its crest swept it from the rocks.

And the cow, uttering a loud bellow, jumped headlong down.

*L*og Entry 10

Before discussing this story, take a few minutes to write your initial response in your log. Begin perhaps with a single word that could describe how you felt at the end of the story. Then follow that word with ideas, tying together things in the story with experiences in your own life to arrive at a sense of the story's meaning for you.

*C*ollaborating

After sharing with your group the meaning the story had for you, focus on the question of the cow's consciousness. Refer to the two hawk poems as you explore the different effects of first person and third person in conveying the inner sense of the animal. Discuss, too, how the story presentation of the cow is different, if you feel it is, from the poems. Is there a sense in which O'Flaherty is poetic? If there is, can you identify what it is about his prose that moves it toward poetry? On the other hand, what did O'Flaherty include in his story that, in your opinion, might have to have been left out had he written it as a poem?

*W*ork in Progress

Re-read your log entries from the beginning of this section, when you explored your relationships with animals. Select one animal that you know something about and have a real interest in and write both of the following assignments in either poetry or prose.

1. Write about an experience you have had when you identified in some way with a bird or another kind of animal. Stay with the

third-person point of view, but present the animal's consciousness, as Jeffers did in "Hurt Hawks" and O'Flaherty did in "The Cow's Death."

2. Using the same experience, get inside the animal's consciousness and write about it from the animal's point of view. Use the "I" to identify the point of view of the animal, as Hughes did in "Hawk Roosting."

Get together with your group again and share your writings with each other. Discuss which piece each of you found easier to write. Which piece do you feel comes closer to presenting the consciousness of the animal? Which reveals more of you? Which do you like better? Explain why for all three questions.

Work in Progress

If you would like to write additional drafts for your folder, try recasting the text.

1. If you wrote in prose, put your descriptions into poetry.

2. If you wrote in poetry, recast the experience in prose.

3. Select one of the poems—"Hurt Hawks" or "Hawk Roosting"— or your own poem and rewrite it as a short story.

4. Rewrite "The Cow's Death" as a poem. Or write about any animal's death in poetry.

5. Change the persona of your poem or prose and write it from this point of view.

Log Entry 11

Write an entry in your log reflecting on how you felt assuming the consciousness of an animal. To what degree do you feel you were successful? Might it be reasonably argued that the only way we can assume an animal's consciousness is to endow the animal with human qualities? If you were to create an animal persona in the future, what might you try that you didn't this time?

Collaborating

From your Work in Progress activity, read two versions of the same experience to your partner or group. Discuss the strengths of each.

- After you have each shared your work, talk about the different demands that prose and poetry make on the writer. For example, prose usually requires fuller descriptions and a more substantial context for the experience. In reading prose, the reader may expect a more comprehensive treatment of the subject. In poetry, however, we expect to find tightly constructed sentences, words that serve more than one function, often metaphorical or symbolic, pushing us to leaps of the imagination.

- Talk about the different demands prose and poetry make on the reader. Do you find it easier to read one than another? If you do, can you figure out why that is?

- Share suggestions for improving your work, and make a decision about which piece you want to revise for your course portfolio.

Acquiring an animal persona

In the following collection of poems, students wrote from the point of view of an animal that they identified with. Dawn Thomas, who wrote "Wilderastabeast," actually lived in Africa when she was a young child and remembers the wildebeests running in migratory herds. Richard Paul chose to write a light-hearted account of being a flea on his dog; Robert McKean never identifies his subject, but you probably will fairly easily. Annick Mebine writes of the quiet but significant moment when a white swan is transformed into a black one.

Wilderastabeast

Dawn Thomas

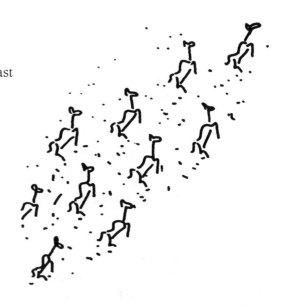

I am a Wildenhmparastabeast
runa
beast
hot hot hot
sunabeatadown
runaruna
beast
grazing on dry grass
nowaterforamillamiles
My People
roundmeinanight
roundmeinaday
My People
wildewildebeast
humpapeople
runaforamillamiles
need a little water
no beef witha People
my brothers
takinanap
innahothotsun
My peoplewatcha
for bigCats
acominround
smelling big beef
My People
oldoldwildebeast
he very tired
Big Cats
achasachasahim
Kill him dead
eatablood
chewachewabones
runapeople
wildeyes arunnin
stampedapeople
too much palaverdust
runafar

runaforawaterhole
only Strongsurviva
underneatha
hot hot hot
sunabeatadown
onmyPeople
My brothers
Wildehumparastabeasta.

The Happy Parasite
Richard Paul

Here I am,
Once again,
Running up and down the spine
Looking for a place to light.

I never have to search around
To find a ripe and tender meal.
I live on life.
That keeps me living.

My dog is really a good guy.
He doesn't bother me too much.
Sometimes a scratch here and
Sometimes a bite there;

It's his people that bother me.
They're always spraying and hunting,
Poking and squeezing.
It drives me to drink!

    So I do.

Oh, I just love to hop around
Amidst the furry jungle.
My feet hardly ever
touch the ground.

I like it this way,
and I want it to stay.
A flea's life is definitely
Not a dog's life.

The Hunter

Robert McKean

Me, black as night,
A king in my own right,
A nightmare to my enemies,
A benefactor to my kin.

My fur is supple and soft;
muscles bunch and flex as
I bound across the open clearings,
then silently fade into the
     surrounding forest searching for prey.

I stop, sniff the air, hoping to catch
     that familiar scent. I run on.
Again I stop. This time my mind pictures
     an old acquaintance, the antelope.

Remorse? Never.
I take what I need, when I need it.
I ignore them when need is absent.
Never more, never less.

Me, black as night,
A king in my own right,
A nightmare to my enemies.
Need is present.

Black Swan

Annick Mebine

The clear pool ripples silently,
mimicking my movements. I have no
bearings, floating effortlessly like
a ball of cotton, white and full,
suspended on the water's surface.

Ahead, near the shore, droplets of
water spatter about as a duck
pointlessly flaps his wings.

Now the glare from the sun becomes
bright. I dip my neck and head
into the cool blueness. In the shade
a green fern wavers in the breeze.

The water is very still and mirrors
the clouds against the sky. I burrow
my face in the downy feathers of my
wing and look at my reflection.

A red bill, but here black feathers
frame it. Black. Moments before,
white. I quickly immerse my whole
body under water, staying there as
long as I can. Finally I swim up.

I look straight at a wet rock that
sat in the center of the pond. From
under it comes a black swan, in the
place where I once was.

Going inside an object

Read the following poem by Charles Simic in which he both gives
and takes his own advice to "go inside a stone."

Stone
Charles Simic

Go inside a stone.
That would be my way.
Let somebody else become a dove
Or gnash with a tiger's tooth.
I am happy to be a stone.

From the outside the stone is a riddle:
No one knows how to answer it.
Yet within, it must be cool and quiet
Even though a cow steps on it full weight,
Even though a child throws it in a river;
The stone sinks, slow, unperturbed
To the river bottom
Where the fishes come to knock on it
And listen.

I have seen sparks fly out
When two stones are rubbed,
So perhaps it is not dark inside after all;
Perhaps there is a moon shining
From somewhere, as though behind a hill—
Just enough light to make out
The strange writings, the star charts
On the inner walls.

Work in Progress

Try taking Simic's advice and go inside some thing from the natural world—a stone, a feather, a shell, a leaf, a drop of water. Notice how Simic makes the world of the stone very particular, with recognizable scenes from the realistic world; yet he also creates a mysterious world with "strange writings," and "star charts/On the inner walls." Write from the inside of the object you choose, either in poetry or prose, and try to convey your imagined world.

Building Your Course Portfolio

You have probably written from many angles of vision and from many points of view other than your own in your classes over the years. You may have written letters from one character to another; recast history into a story or poem told from the point of view of a historical figure; brought a myth into contemporary life and rewritten the story from the mythical figure's point of view; created a science fiction character and imagined a futuristic world. If you've studied debate, you have learned to argue from a point of view you disagree with.

In the first part of this chapter, you experimented with assuming structural forms of both individual writers and established forms of poetry. Then you probed the consciousness of animals and natural objects by adopting their personas. Now we ask you to look at what you have read and what you have written during this chapter and to do some reflecting about what this looking reveals about who you are—not only as a reader and writer but as a unique human being.

The extended portfolio entry, your last project of this chapter, will contain a selection of your writing and your responses to literature. It will represent your best work and will become the basis for an evaluation of your work over this period of time. Review Building Your Course Portfolio in Chapter 1.

Selecting Your Best Writing

Take out your log and your writing folder and look at all the writing you have done during this chapter. Your goal is to select those pieces which you feel represent your best work. Get together with the other members of your writing group so you can help evaluate each other's work; then decide which pieces need revision and which are ready for inclusion. You may want to include some of your log entries as well as the poems, memory writings, stories, or essays that you wrote.

Revising

The word *revise* means, literally, "to see again." To revise a piece of writing requires you to step back, squint your eyes, and look at it a different way. Revising gives you another way to look out through other people's eyes—in this case through the eyes of your readers. You can, of course, revise a piece all by yourself; many writers work this way. But most writers feel the need to have other people read their work, respond honestly to it, ask questions, and let the writer know how the piece affected them.

If you have not worked with a writing group in revising, you might find some starting suggestions helpful. Look over this list and use any of the suggestions that seem pertinent.

- Guide the discussion about your work. Ask questions; probe for detailed responses from the group.

- If possible, make copies of your work for the members of your group. That may not always be possible, but it is helpful.

- Read the piece aloud to the group members (even if they have their own copies), noticing as you read whether there are any sections that you have difficulty reading. If you find such sentences or phrases, come back to them later. Stumbling over a passage while reading aloud may be a clue to the need for re-working that passage.

- Ask the group members to tell you how they felt listening to your piece. Check their reactions against your intent. You may find that they responded in a way that you did not intend but like anyway. Writers build on this kind of knowledge, maybe changing their own concept of their piece as they listen to discussion.

- Ask the group members to talk about point of view. Were you successful in conveying the consciousness of your persona, whether that persona was you, an animal, or another person? Were there any breaks in point of view? If, for example, you were writing from the point of view of a horse, did you maintain that viewpoint throughout?

- If you have any questions about whether you told too much or not enough, ask the members of your group. Where did they need more details? Where did they get bored?

Work on your selected piece until you are satisfied that it is the best you can do; use the suggestions of your teacher and your writing group as you revise. Remember, however, that other people can only give you suggestions. It's up to you as the author to make the final decisions.

Editing

The final step before publishing is checking your work for the kinds of errors that detract from a reader's ability to read for meaning. Look at your work objectively, or get the help of someone in your writing group, and check for spelling, punctuation, and sentence errors. Even after you have made a final copy, you need to proofread for typographical errors. If you use a computer, you can use a spell check, but that won't catch words that are spelled correctly but aren't the words you intended. To proofread your own work, it helps to have some time elapse between the final writing and the proofreading. Our eyes tend to see what our mind intended, regardless of what is in front of them.

Selecting Responses to Your Reading

Include in your portfolio entry an annotated list of titles and authors of poems or stories you found meaningful. Reread the log entries you wrote as you thought about each work. Beside the title of each one, write a short log-type reflective entry indicating why you selected that work. Your reasons may range widely: you may choose one poem because you shared the insight of the author and choose another because it introduced you to a new or unusual perspective. You might like some of the students' work because it is like yours. You might like a piece because you responded to it emotionally or because it let you see some aspect of life through different eyes. You might even choose a piece because it introduced you to a new form, one you tried and liked. Whatever your choices, express some detailed reasons for your responses in your portfolio reading list.

Publishing

If you want to take your work beyond the portfolio, there are many ways to publish your work. Share it with other people—read it aloud, post your work on the bulletin board, put it into a class collection, send it to the school or local newspaper (which may have a weekly poetry section), or submit it to a magazine. There are some magazines that look especially for student writing, hoping to spot young talent. The most important thing is the sharing, however. Be sure to share your favorite work with your family and friends.

Reflecting

When you've made all of your selections—both reading and writing—arrange the pieces in an order that suits you and prepare a Table of Contents. Write an introductory essay on what you've chosen to place in this section of your portfolio and why. This essay should represent your best thinking and writing. It should convey to the readers of your portfolio—other members of your class, your teacher, perhaps friends, and members of your family—who you are at this time of your life in terms of the reading and writing you have done during your work in this chapter.

Because this chapter dealt with helping you explore options—of structures and points of view—we hope that you'll have a somewhat clearer picture of the many possibilities that make up who you are and who you are becoming.

3

Translating a Myth into a Painting, a Painting into a Poem

*M*yths are stories that incorporate important truths about relationships of people to each other, to the earth, to their gods. Ancient myths have been inspirations for artists, musicians, and poets throughout history. Contemporary artists still look to myths as catalysts for their creations. In this chapter, we'll look at a cluster of poems that are derived from the myth of Icarus, the subject of the poem that you read from different angles of vision at the beginning of this book. To understand Daedalus and Icarus more fully, you'll need some additional background. The myth is summarized in the following paragraphs. (If you want to read more about Daedalus's exploits, you will find them in *Metamorphoses,* by the ancient Greek writer Ovid.)

Icarus's father Daedalus was known throughout the ancient world for his inventions and his cleverness. He was proud of his reputation and feared that his young nephew might surpass him. To prevent that from happening, he threw his nephew to his death. Then, to escape punishment for that dreadful act, he fled with his son Icarus to the island of Crete. The king of Crete, King Minos, knowing of Daedalus's cleverness, had him construct a maze to imprison the minotaur, a strange beast that was half-bull and half-man. When Minos used the maze to imprison the hero Theseus (who was in love with Minos's daughter Ariadne) in the maze with the minotaur, Daedalus felt sorry for Ariadne and Theseus and taught Ariadne the secret of how to free Theseus from the maze. King Minos punished Daedalus by imprisoning him and Icarus in the same labyrinth.

The story goes that Daedalus, freed from the maze but still exiled on the island of Crete, was homesick. Knowing that he could not escape by boat, he found himself gazing at the sky, watching the birds, and thinking about how he might engineer his and his son's escape by wings. He began to gather feathers that dropped from great sea birds and then spread them out to make wings, fastening them with twine and wax. When he had constructed wings for himself and his son, he taught his son, the way fathers try to do: "I warn you, Icarus, don't go too low or the water will weigh the wings down and you will be pulled into the sea. Don't go too high or the sun will melt the wax from the feathers and burn the feathers. Steer a middle course and you will be able to fly like the birds and reach the land of your birth. Don't try to chart your own course by the stars or the sun: Follow me. I will lead you safely."

Daedalus kissed his son, then spread his own wings and began to fly over the sea. Icarus followed, beating his wings, flying over the water. Below them, a fisherman watched in amazement, and a shepherd. A ploughman looked up. They could not believe what they saw: a man and a boy, flying high in the sky.

But Icarus, filled with the joy of the flight, flew higher and higher, testing the power of the wings that carried him up into the heavens. He flew high into the sky, nearer and nearer to the sun, until the wax that held the feathers together melted. "Father!" Icarus cried, as he fell from the heavens. "Father!" he cried as he disappeared into the sea.

And Daedalus responded, "Icarus, where are you?" Then he saw the wings on the water and knew that his son had drowned and that all of his ingenuity and inventions could not save the one thing he loved in the world.

Recasting the Myth of Icarus

The yearning to fly, to test and go beyond the limits, has drawn many people to this myth. Painters, dancers, and sculptors throughout history have tried to translate this myth of flying and falling into color and line and movement.

In 1558, a famous painter named Brueghel translated a scene from the myth about Daedalus and Icarus into a painting. Titled *Landscape with the Fall of Icarus,* the painting depicts an everyday scene of people going about their daily lives; the only trace of Icarus is his legs flailing as he goes down into the sea. Brueghel's painting has since become the inspiration for a number of well-known poems. As you read these poems, try to imagine your own picture of Brueghel's painting.

Landscape with the Fall of Icarus
William Carlos Williams

According to Brueghel
when Icarus fell
it was spring

a farmer was ploughing
his field
the whole pageantry

of the year was
awake tingling
near

the edge of the sea
concerned with itself

sweating in the sun
that melted
the wing's wax

insignificantly
off the coast
there was

a splash quite unnoticed
this was
Icarus drowning

In the following poem by the contemporary poet W. H. Auden, you
will not find Icarus mentioned by name until the second stanza.

Musée des Beaux Arts

W. H. Auden

About suffering they were never wrong,
The old Masters: how well they understood
Its human position; how it takes place
While someone else is eating or opening a window or just
     walking dully along;
How, when the aged are reverently, passionately waiting
For the miraculous birth, there always must be
Children who did not specially want it to happen, skating
On a pond at the edge of the wood:
They never forgot
That even the dreadful martyrdom must run its course
Anyhow in a corner, some untidy spot
Where the dogs go on with their doggy life and the
     torturer's horse
Scratches its innocent behind on a tree.

In Brueghel's *Icarus,* for instance: how everything turns
     away
Quite leisurely from the disaster; the ploughman may

Have heard the splash, the forsaken cry,
But for him it was not an important failure; the sun shone
As it had to on the white legs disappearing into the green
Water; and the expensive delicate ship that must have seen
Something amazing, a boy falling out of the sky,
Had somewhere to get to and sailed calmly on.

Tone is a critical factor in all writing but especially in poetry. Try reading this poem aloud; then listen to someone else read it aloud. Listen for the tone. How would you describe it? Resigned? Cynical? Matter-of-fact? Talk with your partner and see whether you agree on how to describe the tone.

The community of thought in the Brueghel-Icarus poems transcends both time and space as painters and writers translate stories and ideas from one historical era to another, making them their own, making the stories relevant to changing perceptions.

*L*og Entry 1

Sketch the outlines of what you think the Brueghel painting must look like, using clues from the poems based on his work. Compare your notes with those of your partner or group. Then find a copy of the painting in an art book and see how closely the poets based their interpretations on Brueghel's painting. (The painting is in many collections. You shouldn't have any difficulty finding a copy in the library.)

Here is another contemporary poet's interpretation of the Icarus myth. This view takes quite a different slant from that of Brueghel or the poets you have read so far. In this poem Edward Field transplants Icarus into present-day society.

Icarus
Edward Field

Only the feathers floating around the hat
Showed that anything more spectacular had occurred
Than the usual drowning. The police preferred to ignore

The confusing aspects of the case,
And the witnesses ran off to a gang war.
So the report filed and forgotten in the archives read
    simply
"Drowned," but it was wrong: Icarus
Had swum away, coming at last to the city
Where he rented a house and tended the garden.

"That nice Mr. Hicks" the neighbors called him,
Never dreaming that the gray, respectable suit
Concealed arms that had controlled huge wings
Nor that those sad, defeated eyes had once
Compelled the sun. And had he told them
They would have answered with a shocked,
    uncomprehending stare.
No, he could not disturb their neat front yards;
Yet all his books insisted that this was a horrible
    mistake:
What was he doing aging in a suburb?
Can the genius of the hero fall
To the middling stature of the merely talented?

And nightly Icarus probes his wound
And daily in his workshop, curtains carefully drawn,
Constructs small wings and tries to fly
To the lighting fixture on the ceiling:
Fails every time and hates himself for trying.

He had thought himself a hero, had acted heroically,
And dreamt of his fall, the tragic fall of the hero;
But now rides commuter trains,
Serves on various committees,
And wishes he had drowned.

*G*raphic

Select any two texts from the Icarus poems or the summary of the
myth that you have read and draw your responses to them. Look to
the texts for visual scenes and translate them into sketches; try to

sketch how these texts affected you as well as what you think the meaning is. Include representations of connections between your own life and that of the Icarus of the texts. Are you more like the Icarus of the myth, defying his father, flying for the joy of testing his own power, or like the Icarus of the Field poem, regretting that his one heroic moment did not end in glory but in a boring, mundane life? Let your drawing convey your interpretations and feelings.

Collaborating

With your partner or group, talk about the different versions of the Icarus myth. Here are some general questions for starters:

- Which poem caused your strongest reaction?

- What events seemed strange or out of place?

- What actions of Icarus seemed hard to explain?

- Were you reminded of any personal experiences as you read about Icarus defying his father?

- What ideas did the poems make you think about?

With regard to Edward Field's poem, discuss these questions:

- How do you interpret the lines "Can the genius of the hero fall/To the middling stature of the merely talented?" In what way do you think Edward Field might see Icarus as a genius, a tragic hero?

- Icarus, in Field's poem, sees himself as having been a man who "acted heroically,/And dreamt of his fall, the tragic fall of the hero." Think of some of the tragedies you have read—Shakespeare's *Macbeth* or *Hamlet* or Sophocles' *Oedipus* (which appears later in this book)—and talk about Field's use of the concept of the "tragic fall" with respect to Icarus. Remember that in reading a myth, each person projects details into the story that make it relevant to his or her own situation.

One student, who was grieving a lost mother-son relationship in his own life, identified strongly with the fallen Icarus. In his poem, however, he chose to speak with the voice of the stricken mother, who does not appear in the myth, imagining, perhaps, that his own mother would have such feelings. Here is Bill's poem, written his senior year. Read it aloud in your group.

Icarus

Bill Whiteman

Icarus, come with me.
I feel small wings
growing from my womb.
Let us walk beside the sea.
Let us taste the flesh
of freshly fallen seabirds.
Let us feel the tender oils
of Grecian mermaids.
Icarus, come with me.
The sun will never touch us
with its too many fingers
of light.
We can watch the moon
with its silent albino ponies.
Icarus, I want you
to travel with me forever.
I want you to come
and walk beside metal barges
that have eroded into the tide.
I want to comb your tired feathers.
Let me brush your solemn wings.
Icarus, come with me,
come with me.

My child has fallen.
His wings have melted
into summer clouds.
His eyes have grown soft
from looking at the sun too long.
His once-beautiful blonde feathers
have grown dark and dull.

Icarus, why did you try
to make love with the sun,
with its evil chariot,
with its mirrored beauty?
You should have come with me, Icarus,
I loved you.

Collaborating

What are your initial reactions to Bill's poem? About the whole
process of rewriting myths into contemporary versions? Retelling a
myth in the language of one's own time is one thing, but actually
changing the story, as Edward Field does, is another. Select a myth
you know—a Greek myth, an Indian myth, a Norse myth, or a contemporary myth such as the story of Superman—and talk with your
partner or group about how you might "translate" or rewrite it to
make a statement about some aspect of society today.

Recasting Other Myths

Following is a revised version of the myth of Prometheus, whose
name means, literally, "forethought." Barry Tribuzio was inspired to
write this untitled poem during his senior year in high school after
reading Edward Field's poem, "Icarus."

Barry Tribuzio

But he has made the true
escape from reality's pain
to consolidated gain,
His name etched in brass
and his life in code
on a chip stored away,
He is no more loved here
than caressed by the talons
and cold hard rock.

Eaten up inside by
the schedules of life,
Broken by the whip
of market trends,
"Time is Money"
and the clocks on the wall.

But these things
do not occur to him;
He sullenly scratches
the healing itch of his belly
and calls for coffee.
Ankles bound in shined shoes
He reclines,
lost in the grasp
of padded vinyl,
And the pigeons gather
outside for a feast . . .

Chris Walton, another student inspired by Field's poem, wrote a modern version of the story of Daphne and Apollo (Philip in the poem). Daphne was a nymph who, when pursued by Apollo, chose to be turned into a bay tree and consecrated to Apollo.

Wooded Lovers

Chris Walton

Quietly they left when
They ran away to Marin
And became the happiest
And the oddest couple on the block.
They didn't tell anyone she was supposed to be a tree.

Daphne and Philip live normal lives:
She leads Girl Scouts through the woods
Like some kind of huntress;
He plays the harp expertly
For the San Francisco Symphony
And heads the campaign to "Save the Dolphins."

Still, they are unable to escape
Destiny and the curse from her father.

Once born, their children grow leaves
And become part of their laurel forest.
The neighbors joke, "They stay married
Because of the children—the lack of them."
Daphne and Philip laugh, and inside
they envy their fertile friends.

At night she lies awake,
Sorry her father's spell missed her,
Longing to join her children in nature.
Next to her Philip grows old,
Hates himself for falling in love.

But they love eternally,
Their bond too beautiful, too strong to break;
the hidden despair in the suburbs and
Frustration of old age is not enough
To erase the wonder of life:
They live on.

*E*xtending the Myth of Icarus

"Modern mythology recognizes both the upward and the downward impulse in human nature," writes F. Parvin Sharpless in *Symbol and Myth in Modern Literature* (Rochelle Park, N.J.: Hayden Book Co., 1976). You have seen, in the myth of Icarus, the imagery of the air and sun—the upward movement—and of the earth and water—the downward pull. But the drama of the story often lies in the passage between—the rising and the falling, not only of a boy who, flying too near the sun, falls into the sea, but of basic aspects of human nature to aspire, to fall, to rise again.

Icarus is only one of a number of Greek myths that have given rise to artists' and writers' translations over the years. Following are some suggestions for you, working either alone or with a partner, to extend your own understanding of myth. Through these activities, you can begin to develop your own consciousness of how myths—through the arts of painting, poetry, and drama—reflect aspects of what it means to be a human being.

Many writers and artists have seen Icarus as the perpetual adolescent. Reread the original version of the story of Daedalus and

Icarus (see pages 74–75); look again at the Brueghel painting and reread the cluster of Icarus poems. Think about times in your life when you have defied the limits implicit in being young. Think about the consequences of your defiance. Then try some of the following possibilities for pieces to include in your writing folder. Remember that later you may want to revise one or more to include in your course portfolio.

*W*ork in Progress

- *Write a reflective-analytic essay.* Write about how you perceive the Icarus story and why you think the myth continues to influence artists and writers. Look specifically at how Ovid influenced Brueghel, Auden, Williams, Field, Sexton (from Chapter 1), and the student, Bill Whiteman. Be specific in your references to the poems, drawing on lines or forms or images that illustrate your ideas. Reflect on the continuing power of the Icarus myth to affect different artists in different time periods.

- *Recast the text into a nonverbal art form.* Translate the Icarus myth into some art form: a painting, a collage, a mandala, a sculpture. Or you could write the words and music for a song based on the theme of Icarus or compose a dance that carries the theme of flying and falling.

- *Research a myth—outwardly and inwardly.* Select the story of a different mythic figure and track down all the translations you can find in art, music, drama, or poetry. Create your own translation of this myth in any art form. Then write a short account of the process of your investigation and your creation.

- *Update a myth.* Select a myth that says something important to you and rewrite it to reflect a truth you see in society today. Write it as a poem or story or play. (See the poems in this chapter by Barry Tribuzio and Chris Walton for examples of myths rewritten as modern poems.) Write an entry in your log explaining why you chose your myth and why you made the changes in the myth that you did.

- *Read a mythic extension.* Because myths carry a deep significance for people of every era, the stories of the myths appear and reappear in different cultures and in different settings, with outwardly different situations. If you are ambitious, you might want to try reading a sustained treatment of a myth in a novel or play. There are many to choose from. We suggest four possible selections. If everyone in your group reads the same work, you will be able to talk about the ideas and issues each writer explores.

  Portrait of the Artist as a Young Man by James Joyce is a short novel that grows out of the Daedalus/Icarus myth. The young man in the novel is named Stephen Daedalus, although at times he is more like Icarus than Daedalus. This is not an easy book to read, but it is worth your while if you like probing ideas and experiencing inventive use of language. It leads to a lot of good discussion about growing up, especially about a young boy/man who isn't part of the crowd and whose artistic temperament sets him apart from the rough-and-tumble lives of his schoolmates.

  The Centaur by John Updike is a wonderful experiment in writing a novel on two levels at the same time. On one level, it is the story of three days in the life of a high school history teacher/coach (Chiron, the centaur) and his son Peter (Prometheus). Zimmerman, the principal of the high school, is, of course, Zeus; and Vera Hummel, the women's physical education teacher, is Venus, and so on. On the other hand, interspersed throughout the novel are vignettes of myths about the main characters' mythic counterparts—primarily Chiron, the centaur, but others, as well. You can read the book for the story alone, but you will find yourself drawn into the ramifications of myths as stories about our most powerful feelings and ideas.

  Read two plays based on the same Greek story—the story of Antigone, daughter of Oedipus. Sophocles' *Antigone* is the third play in the trilogy of plays about Oedipus (the first play, *Oedipus Rex,* appears later in this book). The power of *Antigone* lies in the confrontation between Antigone, the young, fiercely free-thinking daughter of Oedipus, and her uncle, now king, Creon. Antigone chooses to go to her death for burying her brother against the laws of the state rather than give in to what she believes are unjust laws. Jean Anouilh, a French dramatist of this

century, wrote his dramatic version of *Antigone* as a symbolic enactment of the German occupation of France during World War II. The parallels are clear; the drama is compelling. After reading these two plays, you might want to write your own version of Antigone's story, selecting someone from contemporary history to fulfill the role of Antigone, the defiant young challenger of the establishment. In the 1960s, students chose folk singer Joan Baez to embody the Antigone idealism. Can you think of current performers, public figures, or other people who exemplify Antigone's beliefs?

4

Truth in Fiction

*P*eople like to classify things, to give them names and categories, to separate one kind of bird or car or tree from another. We're used to classification in science; an eighteenth-century Swedish botanist named Linnaeus formulated a classification system that we still use today. Because of Linnaeus's work, a botanist, seeing an unnamed plant, for example, could immediately classify it according to its class, order, family, genus, and species. When you know what the scientific name is for a plant, you know something about it—what other plants it's related to and, therefore, how it fits into the larger picture of the plant kingdom. Even in biology there are problems, however. For example, the euglena, a microscopic bit of something, has chlorophyll in it, a definitive characteristic of the plant kingdom; it also is able to initiate movement, a definitive characteristic of the animal kingdom. So which is it, plant or animal?

Of course, it is false logic to maintain that where boundaries are blurred, no distinctions exist. Just because no one can specify at which smudge a clean wall becomes a dirty wall, that does not mean there is no difference between a clean wall and a dirty wall.

*C*lassifying Literature

English teachers and critics have followed the lead of Linnaeus and over the years have tried to classify kinds of literature and kinds of writing. We even use the word *genre,* which is related to the scientific term *genus,* to distinguish categories of literature—the novel, the essay, the poem, and so on. Each is considered a separate genre, with descriptive qualities that help us identify the differences among types. But we run into trouble with our own euglenas. "What is poetry, and if you know what poetry is, what is prose?" asks Gertrude Stein, a noted poet of the 1930s and 40s.

Two big categories of writing, almost as large as the plant and animal kingdoms, seemed pretty clear-cut for a long time: fiction and nonfiction. You have probably already learned what these useful categories mean and how they are distinct from one another.

Before you go on, take a minute to write in your log simple definitions of *fiction* and *nonfiction* as you understand them. This is not a trap; it's just a way of getting started.

*L*og Entry 1

Define fiction and nonfiction. Don't look them up in the dictionary; just define these words as you might use them. Write out a working definition for each one.

*C*ollaborating

Share your definitions with your group and talk about the different ways you approached defining these words. Did you

- use the words *true* or *false* or perhaps *made up?*

- write statements of definition?

- use examples?

- define by using similes or metaphors ("fiction is like . . .")?

How were each of your definitions different from one another? If you want to add anything to your definitions or perhaps change them, write your additions in your log now.

We will come back to this discussion after you have read a few pieces of literature. First read the opening lines of the autobiographical reminiscences of Doctor Robert Coles in "Starting Out."

> The youth of fifteen had polio; he would lose the use of both legs. His father had been killed in the Second World War; his mother had died in an automobile accident when he was ten. A grandmother, a sensitive and thoughtful widow in her sixties, had become his main family. The young man had no brothers and sisters. He had two uncles, whom he yearned to see more often, but they were living in Texas and California.

*L*og Entry 2

Write in your log how you think you might feel if you were in this young man's situation: fifteen, orphaned, facing the rest of your life without the use of your legs. Try writing as if you were this person. You might include sketches or drawings that this young person might draw to represent his life.

The narrator of "Starting Out" is a pediatrician and child psychiatrist. He begins by interviewing the young man as part of his study of young polio victims. Now read the rest of the excerpt.

Starting Out
Robert Coles

The youth of fifteen had polio; he would lose the use of both legs. His father had been killed in the Second World War; his mother had died in an automobile accident when he was ten. A grandmother, a sensitive and thoughtful widow in her sixties, had become his main family. The young man had no brothers and sisters. He had two uncles, whom he yearned to see more often, but they were living in Texas and California. (Like him, they were born near Boston.) I came to know this fellow fairly well. I first met him in the emergency ward of a Boston hospital when he came in with a sore throat, feverish, and, alas, weak in the legs. My work with him as a pediatrician gave way eventually to my conversations with him as a child psychiatrist. He was "moody," by his own description, and he was not averse to long talks.

We always started with sports, especially baseball and hockey, his two loves. In time, we'd drift toward the hospital scene as he saw it: the nurses, the virtues and faults of various ones, and the doctors, mostly their faults. He regarded us residents with a skeptical eye. We strutted, were all too cocky. "The doctors give so many orders, it goes to their heads." He said those words so many times that I found myself, in retaliation, observing his "hostility." It was hard for him to accept the bad deal life had given him. He was angry, I knew, and needed a target, someone or something to attack, lest he turn all the fury on himself and become depressed. As he described us doctors, scurrying around, always on the move, collaring people with our orders, he seemed wistful. He would look past me, toward a window, and I always hesitated to press our conversation. He seemed gone—his mind was out there, free of his body.

Once, as we talked about that body's prospects, he became philosophical. He wondered whether the soul is always confined to a given body. Might it become migratory? What did I think? I was stupid enough to shun the question and to throw it back at him. He was smart enough to spot my pose—a shrink in action—and irritated enough to give me a dose of his bile. He spoke at considerable length; one remark has stuck with me for the many years since he made it: "If you would tell me what you think, then I could answer better." At the time I wasn't getting any wiser, however. I interpreted that comment as an effort on his part to hide behind me, as it were—to let me know that he would pretend to oblige me by taking cues from me, but not deliver to me what I wanted, his own unvarnished self. He spotted a coy reserve in me at that moment, which must have told him what was crossing my mind. He changed the subject abruptly, instructively. Had I read *The Adventures of Huckleberry Finn*? Yes, I answered, wondering what the question meant. He said no more. It was left to me, during the silence that followed, to figure out what to say, if anything. I waited just long enough to realize that the youth, whose name was Phil, had no intention of proceeding further in any direction. My wife's and supervisors' faces, their voices, rushed to my head. A week or so earlier my wife had urged me to "exchange stories" with the children I was interviewing in the hospital; Dr. Ludwig had agreed: "Why don't you chuck the word 'interview,' call yourself a friend, call your exchanges 'conversations'!"

Suddenly I heard myself talking about Huck and Jim, about the mighty river, about my own experiences as a child when my mother took my brother and me to visit her family in Sioux City, Iowa, located on the Missouri River. I told Phil that my grandfather used to take me to that river, point south, indicate the destination of the water: the Mississippi, then New Orleans and the ocean. "Those rivers are arteries of the American heartland," he'd tell me—the farmland expanding and contracting, opening up and offering crops, then retreating into the winter lair, and all the while the water flowing, keeping an entire region alive and fertile.

Not brilliant imagery, but enough to shed me of my scrutinizing, wary reticence; enough to involve Phil in a bit of a personal story, which in turn was connected to a reading experience he had recently had, and one I had also had, though about seven or eight years earlier. I was almost ready to tell him how young he was to have read the Mark Twain book—to patronize him foolishly and smugly—when Phil began talking about the book. He had read it as a school assignment before he fell sick. When he'd been in the hospital a week or so and began to realize that he was "really paralyzed" and that his disease might be "for a lifetime," he became morose, more so than others on the same ward with the same disease, for whom the bad news had yet to sink in. All he could think of was "the black space" of his future life. But a teacher came to visit him on a Saturday afternoon, and the result was a reacquaintance with the Twain classic. Not that young Phil relished the idea at first. Here is how he described what happened (his remarks have been edited and on occasion reconstructed because my tape recorder intermittently broke down):

"I was surprised to see him [the teacher]. I'd liked him, but he was gone from my life, the way a teacher is when you go on to the next year of school. I guess he heard I was sick. We all knew he was a softie! Some of those teachers don't give a damn for you as a person. They talk to the back wall, and if you hear, fine, and if you don't, you flunk! This guy we all knew—he was different. I guess I didn't learn how different until he showed up here.

"He came in and smiled and said hello. I was surprised. I said hello back. I didn't have anything more to say, though. He was quiet, too. I was glad! I was tired of people coming and expecting me to talk with them. I wanted to lie there and think. I felt like crying, but I didn't; I couldn't; I think I was afraid that if I started—once I started, I'd never stop. He just sat there and smiled; then he asked if he could go get me something—food, or a glass of juice. I was thirsty, and I said, 'Yes, orange juice'; and he left, and came back with orange juice and with some peanuts. I liked that, the peanuts. I used to nibble on them a lot before I got sick. I remember my mother saying they were better for me than chocolate. I got a little choked up then, thinking of her and the peanuts and looking at my legs. No more baseball. No more hockey. No more walking, either.

"I saw him looking at the magazines I had on the table near my bed. He leafed through them; then he asked me if he could bring me some books, maybe. I shook my head. I didn't want any books. I was beginning to think I didn't want any teachers here either—*him*. Then he said he was going to go! I guess he'd read me! I felt like I was going to cry, but I didn't know why. I was afraid of breaking down in front of him. I tried to tough it out. I became flip. I joked about having a ball when I came back to school—speeding down the corridors at sixty in a wheelchair. He smiled, but he didn't laugh as much as I did. I knew when I was laughing that it was fake. In a minute he was gone—and then I did cry. I didn't even want to see another day. It was raining outside, and I was crying, and my legs were useless, and I haven't even graduated from high school, that's how young I am, and all I can see ahead is those rehabilitation people, and nurses, and my grandmother looking so worried, and she looked so sick, once I got sick. For a while I thought she was going to die, and then there'd be no one.

"He came back a few days later; he had this book under his arm. He didn't push it on me. He stood there and talked, small talk, and I talked. After a few minutes there was nothing more to say. Suddenly, without saying anything, he up and left. I thought it was strange, the way he left. But he hadn't left; I mean, he came back. He had orange juice in one hand, a glass, and peanuts in the other. I couldn't help smiling. That was the first smile on my face, I think, since he'd been to see me. We talked a few minutes more, about the lousy weather, and then he said he was going. He shook my hand, and just as he was saying good-bye, he took the book from under his left arm with his right hand and put it on my table. He didn't say anything, and he was out of the room before I could say anything.

"I was really curious to see which book he'd brought. I looked, and saw it was the Mark Twain one, *Adventures of Huckleberry Finn*. I started flipping through the pages. I wondered why he brought it. I'd already read it—in his class, last year. What was the point? I guess I was a little annoyed with him. I wondered what was wrong with him, at first. Why that book? What's he got in mind? I asked myself those kinds of questions. I didn't go near the book for a few days. It was just there, with the magazines my grandma brought. I didn't read them much either. I'd look at the pictures, and I'd read a paragraph—and you know what? I'd get sick to my stomach. I'd feel like puking. I thought it was part of the sickness. I told the nurse, and she told the doctor, and he asked me, and I explained to him what was going on. He examined me, and told me it was all in my head. I joked with him: I said, 'All'?

"When the doctor left the room, I decided to pick up that book; so I did. I flipped through the pages, and then I started reading it, and then I didn't want to stop. I read and I read, and I finished the whole book that night; it was midnight, maybe. The nurse kept coming in to tell me I should put my light off and go to sleep because I needed my rest. What a joke! Are you kidding! I said to her. I'm going nowhere. I'll be in bed for the rest of my life. What difference does it make to me, night and day? She backed off. I read, and when I was done with the story, I felt different. It's hard to say what I mean. [*What do you think happened?*] I can't tell you, I can't explain what happened; I know that my mind changed after I read *Huckleberry Finn.* I couldn't get my mind off the book. I forgot about myself—no, I didn't, actually. I joined up with Huck and Jim; we became a trio. They were very nice to me. I explored the Mississippi with them on the boats and on the land. I had some good talks with them. I dreamed about them. I'd wake up, and I'd know I'd just been out west, on the Mississippi. I talked with those guys, and they straightened me out!"

At that point he paused for a long time. He shook his head. He stared out the window. Then he abruptly put a question to me: "Have you ever read a book that really made a difference to you—a book you couldn't get out of your mind, and you didn't want to [get out of your mind]?"

Yes, I said, and knowing he wanted an example, I told him: *Paterson,* William Carlos Williams's long poem. We got into a long talk about Dr. Williams's medical work with mostly poor and working-class people and about his effort through stories and poems to understand America's social history and moral values. He asked for examples, which of course I didn't have on hand. But he was obviously setting the stage for another conversation. I got my Williams books out of a box, brought a couple of them to his room the next day, and read from the first two books of *Paterson* and from various poems Williams had published in the course of his long writing life. I will never forget the direction of our discussion afterward. Phil wondered whether Williams would ever have been able to accomplish what he did, were he not inspired by what he was all the time as a practicing physician. Then he wondered whether Mark Twain, whose life he had briefly studied, would have been able to do the kind of writing *he* did, had he not been such an inveterate wanderer before he found himself having much to say. The reason for Phil's interest in pointing out the connection between art and life was not too hard for me to comprehend—or for him, either.

He began musing out loud about his future prospects, with discouragement and dismay. In reply, I pointed out that writers are constantly creating their own worlds, not necessarily needing to travel far and wide in order to gather the particulars for so doing. He once more wanted examples, and our next minutes were taken up with Jane Austen and *Pride and Prejudice,* which I'd read in high school and which his closest friend, a year older, was about to read at the behest of an English teacher. Well, Jane Austen was a novelist, a writer—lucky to be able to achieve what she did, living the life she did. Things would be different for him. He was no writer, would be no writer, had never even thought of becoming one. Now, significantly paralyzed, he could not even be the day-to-day athlete he'd been; nor did books seem the most inviting of alternatives. He politely but firmly reminded me that he was not "the greatest of students," that he was a "slow reader," that he was struggling with his own worries and terrors, not those described by a novelist in a story: "I wish one of those writers had written about the mess I'm in!"

I did not, then, try to come up with a novel that might pass his muster. Even if I had known of a novel with a polio victim of his age, sex, and background as the hero, I would not have mentioned it at the time. His complaint went deeper; like Job, he was puzzled in the most profound way possible and wanted to find his own voice, use it to make his own plea, his own cry, though he had already begun to regard the world as largely indifferent to him and his situation. I decided to await his decision: whether to do some reading as a means of reflecting indirectly, but with emotional resonance, on his personal situation; or to reject such a way of trying to come to terms with his ongoing situation. A week later, as I was talking with him in his room, I noticed a new box of candy on his bedside table, and underneath the candy box a book. The title was not immediately obvious; I had to move toward the window on a pretext—a bit of sun in my eyes, so best to pull the shades. As I did so, I saw that the book was *The Catcher in the Rye.* I didn't say anything; neither did Phil.

A few days later, as we talked about the rehabilitation efforts taking place, Phil suddenly changed the subject: "I've discovered a book that has a kid in it like Huckleberry Finn." I said nothing but looked interested. He asked me, "Have you ever read *The Catcher in the Rye*?" Yes, I answered. "Do you see what I mean about Huck Finn and Holden Caulfield?" Yes, I answered. Silence. I got alarmed.

Why wasn't I feeding our conversation? Why my terse yes, two times spoken? But he began a lively monologue on that novel, on Holden, on Pencey Prep, on "phonies," on what it means to be honest and decent in a world full of "phoniness." Holden's voice (Salinger's) had become Phil's, and uncannily, Holden's dreams of escape, of rescue (to save not only himself but others), became Phil's. The novel had, as he put it, "got" to him: lent itself to his purposes as one who was "flat out"; and as one who was wondering what in life he might "try to catch." He lived on a city street rather than near a field of rye. He was not as utopian, anyway, as Holden. But this youth had been removed by dint of circumstances from the "regular road" (his expression) and he was trying hard to imagine where to go, how to get there. *The Catcher in the Rye* enabled him to return at least to the idea of school—to consider what kind of education he wanted, given his special difficulties.

He had been getting some tutoring in the rehabilitation unit of the hospital. Now he began teaching himself—leaving the building for Huck and Jim on the Mississippi, for repeated excursions to meet Holden. A friend of his invited him to expand his travels, to visit Ralph and Piggy and Jack and Simon on the tropical island in William Golding's *Lord of the Flies*. But Phil resisted that invitation; the book, brought to him by the friend, remained unread. He had glanced at it, seen its charged symbolism, its mix of hard realism and surrealism. Huck and Holden stirred him, brought him to reflection; Ralph and the band of boys on the island were "not for me." When Phil said that, he looked at me and saw my curiosity rising; he decided to give me a terse explication, one I would never forget: "I'd like to leave this hospital, and find a friend or two, and a place where we could be happy, but I don't want to leave the whole world I know."

My wife was quite taken by Phil's way of putting those books into a perspective that suited him. He was calling on certain novels in his own manner and turning away from others for his own reasons. (Phil also rejected the detective stories his friends brought to him, and the Westerns.) A week or so later I heard him again talk about Huck and Jim and Holden. They had become, for him, a threesome. Rather, he had joined them; they were a foursome. His misfortune had evoked in him a wry, sardonic side. He was quick to notice hypocrisy or deceit in the world as it came to him—on television, in the newspapers, in reports from friends and family members, and through hospital personnel. One particular doctor especially offended him, reminding him of a certain teacher and also of an uncle, his mother's older brother. They all "pretended to be nice," but were (in his judgment) "phonies." How he loved that word; what palpable pleasure it gave him! Once, using it, he must have noticed something cross my face—an expression in my eyes, a tightening of my face—and he must have guessed that I thought his use of the word was significant and perhaps inappropriate. He called me on my heightened response to the word "phony"; he told me that both Twain and Salinger were warning the reader to take a hard, close look at the world. If I did so; if I read those two books as he had recently done; if I would "stop and think," then a recognition would descend upon me, too—or so he hoped. He loved the blunt, earthy talk of Twain, and Salinger's shrewd way of puncturing various balloons. He didn't like being paralyzed; but he did like an emerging angle of vision in himself, and he was eager to tell me about it, to explain its paradoxical relationship to his misfortune: "I've seen a lot, lying here. I think I know more about people, including me, myself—all because I got sick and can't walk. It's hard to figure out, how polio can be a good thing. It's not, but I like those books, and I keep reading them, parts of them, over and over."

Log Entry 3

Use the double-entry log format as you reread this piece. Select at least five quotations from the story that you feel strongly enough about to respond to. Think of your work in this log as having a dialogue with the text—with either the young man or the psychiatrist. You might write directly to the speaker of the quotation, expressing your own thoughts, feelings, and fears.

*Co*llaborating

As a group, explore your ideas about Phil, his feelings about the characters in the books, and the way he is dealing with his life. Use your double-entry log as a springboard for your discussion with your group. Share your own responses—incidents in your own life that this story made you remember, or fears you have about your own futures.

Work in Progress

Select one or more of the following options to draft a piece for your writing folder.

- Reflect on some of Phil's philosophical questions, perhaps in a dialogue with him. For example, Phil "wondered whether the soul is always confined to a given body. Might it become migratory?"

- Phil has some critical things to say about "some of those teachers [who] don't give a damn for you as a person." The teacher who comes to see Phil is different, though. Write about a teacher you have had who either showed in some way that she or he really cared about you as a person or one that you feel didn't care about you or your classmates.

- If you have ever established a strong bond with a character from a book, write about it. What was it about the character that led to this bond? Include the circumstances that made this particular character important to you at a specific time in your life.

- Robert Coles, the author of this reminiscence, writes at the end, "He didn't like being paralyzed; but he did like an emerging angle of vision in himself." In this textbook, we ask you to be aware of angles of vision, to try out different angles and see how your perspective changes. Think of something that has happened in your own life that has given you an "emerging angle of vision" about yourself. Write about what it was that happened and how it changed your angle of vision about yourself or your life.

Artistic Truth and Factual Truth

The relationship between a writer's life and the stories he or she creates is often apparent to one who knows the details of the writer's life. To most of us, however, this relationship is not so clear.

Certainly it is a question writers hear over and over again, and sometimes even they are baffled by where their ideas come from. Poets, as well as story writers and novelists, often take liberties with the "factual" details of their lives that become part of their poems. As readers, we do not know, nor should it matter, whether the occasion of the poem actually happened or not. If it did indeed happen, we do not know whether it happened in the same way that it is depicted in the poem. The artistic truth of the work lies much deeper than the factual truth of history or autobiography.

Desmond Chin, when he was a high school senior, wrote this poem about a visit to his grandmother. Remember, the details are true, whether or not they are factual.

Without Words
Desmond Chin

It was a cloudy day,
One of those days which made me feel heavy
And dark inside
Like a puddle of muddy, black water
Which just sits in the middle of a road,
Stagnant and lifeless.

It was always like this
Whenever I came to visit my grandmother
At the convalescent home.
The wind would always bite,
almost as if it knew that
It was just so depressing
And so hopeless.

She was in room 6,
Sitting in a chair,
Rocking back and forth, unceasingly.
She wasn't always like this.
She used to be energetic,
With hands attracted to paper work.

But things changed
Once the disease
Began eating away at her mind.
Day by day, I noticed the change.
She forgot numbers, dates, months,
And then she forgot me.

"Hi, Grandma! Do you remember me?
I'm your grandson,
The one who you thought
Was the President of the United States.
Do you remember me?"
She just sat there,
Her eyes looking at me,
And then looking away.

I held her frail, bony hand.
There was no warmth in the fingers,
Only coldness like frozen ice
And hardness like a mass of solid rock,
But they were my grandma's hands,
Hands that had once held me
When I was a little baby,
Hands that had held my hands
When I was learning to walk.

"Grandma. Do you remember me?
It's your grandson."

I was hoping some faint tear
Would answer me, But she just sat in the room,
Staring ahead at nothing,
Not able to recognize the wall in front of her
Or me, whenever I came to visit her.

Work in Progress

Choose one or more of the following options to draft for your writing folder.

- Write a dialogue between yourself and Desmond in which you share an experience that has given each of you a deeper understanding of a family member as a person.

- Robert Cormier, author of *Eight Plus One,* a collection of stories that has grown out of his own experiences, wrote in his introduction to "The Moustache," "I tell people that my ideas usually grow out of an emotion—something I have experienced, observed, or felt. The emotion sparks my impulse to write and I find myself at the typewriter trying to get the emotion and its impact down on paper. Out of that comes a character and then a plot. The sequence seldom varies: emotion, character, plot."

Think of an experience you have had that could provide the nonfiction seed for a fictional story or poem. Make some notes about the emotion you felt about this experience; then create a character, someone other than yourself, and see how this character enters into that experience. Write as much as you can about how this situation might play out. Later you may want to develop this idea into a full-fledged story.

- Write notes for a poem fictionalizing the same experience you recalled in the previous assignment.

- Make some observations comparing the writing of a story and a poem. Note the relative importance of emotion, character, and plot in the two different pieces you have made notes for or drafted.

A Short Story and Its Origin

Henry James, an influential British novelist of the late nineteenth and early twentieth centuries, once commented that simply walking past a drawing room without even pausing to overhear a snatch of conversation was all one needed to stimulate the writing of a novel. That's all anyone needs; the rest is already inside us.

The next story, about an old woman named Phoenix Jackson, was stimulated by such a simple observation. Eudora Welty, the author of "A Worn Path," writes, "One day I saw a solitary old woman like Phoenix. She was walking. I saw her, at middle distance, in a winter country landscape, and watched her slowly make her way across my line of vision. That sight of her made me write the story." After you read the story, you will read more about the writer's own ideas about it and look again at the shifting lines of distinction between nonfiction, what we think of as the truth of the matter, and fiction, what we often think of as made up or created out of the imagination.

Begin by having someone read aloud the first two paragraphs, which follow, of Welty's story for the class or for your group.

It was December—a bright frozen day in the early morning. Far out in the country there was an old Negro woman with her head tied in a red rag, coming along a path through the pinewoods. Her name was Phoenix Jackson. She was very old and small and she walked slowly in the dark pine shadows, moving a little from side to side in her steps, with the balanced heaviness and lightness of a pendulum in a grandfather clock. She carried a thin, small cane made from an umbrella, and with this she kept tapping the frozen earth in front of her. This made a grave and persistent noise in the still air, that seemed meditative like the chirping of a solitary little bird.

She wore a dark striped dress reaching down to her shoe tops, and an equally long apron of bleached sugar sacks, with a full pocket: all neat and tidy, but every time she took a step she might have fallen over her shoelaces, which dragged from her unlaced shoes. She looked straight ahead. Her eyes were blue with age. Her skin had a pattern all its own of numberless branching wrinkles and as though a whole little tree stood in the middle of her forehead, but a golden color ran underneath, and the two knobs of her cheeks were illumined by a yellow burning under the dark. Under the red rag her hair came down on her neck in the frailest of ringlets, still black, and with an odor like copper.

Log Entry 4

Imagining or picturing is central to your reading. Without looking back at these two paragraphs, try sketching or drawing this opening scene as you heard or read it the first time. Go back to the text and, as you reread, fill in details of your sketch that you missed on the first reading. Notice where your attention was on the first reading: Was it primarily focused on Phoenix Jackson and how she was dressed? On details of her eyes and skin? Were you aware of the kind of country she was walking through? Were you reminded of anyone you have known or seen? Around your sketch, jot down words that describe your impressions of Phoenix. Now, begin again at the beginning and read the entire story.

A Worn Path
by Eudora Welty

It was December—a bright frozen day in the early morning. Far out in the country there was an old Negro woman with her head tied in a red rag, coming along a path through the pinewoods. Her name was Phoenix Jackson. She was very old and small and she walked slowly in the dark pine shadows, moving a little from side to side in her steps, with the balanced heaviness and lightness of a pendulum in a grandfather clock. She carried a thin, small cane made from an umbrella, and with this she kept tapping the frozen earth in front of her. This made a grave and persistent noise in the still air, that seemed meditative like the chirping of a solitary little bird.

She wore a dark striped dress reaching down to her shoe tops, and an equally long apron of bleached sugar sacks, with a full pocket: all neat and tidy, but every time she took a step she might have fallen over her shoelaces, which dragged from her unlaced shoes. She looked straight ahead. Her eyes were blue with age. Her skin had a pattern all its own of numberless branching wrinkles and as though a whole little tree stood in the middle of her fore-head, but a golden color ran underneath, and the two knobs of her cheeks were illumined by a yellow burning under the dark. Under the red rag her hair came down on her neck in the frailest of ringlets, still black, and with an odor like copper.

Now and then there was a quivering in the thicket. Old Phoenix said, "Out of my way, all you foxes, owls, beetles, jack rabbits, coons and wild animals! . . . Keep out from under these feet, little bob-whites . . . Keep the big wild hogs out of my path. Don't let none of those come running my direction. I got a long way." Under her small black-freckled hand her cane, limber as a buggy whip, would switch at the brush as if to rouse up any hiding things.

On she went. The woods were deep and still. The sun made the pine needles almost too bright to look at, up where the wind rocked. The cones dropped as light as feathers. Down in the hollow was the mourning dove—it was not too late for him.

The path ran up a hill. "Seems like there is chains about my feet, time I get this far," she said, in the voice of argument old people keep to use with themselves. "Something always take a hold of me on this hill—pleads, I should say."

After she got to the top she turned and gave a full, severe look behind her where she had come. "Up through pines," she said at length. "Now down through oaks."

Her eyes opened their widest, and she started down gently. But before she got to the bottom of the hill a bush caught her dress.

Her fingers were busy and intent, but her skirts were full and long, so that before she could pull them free in one place they were caught in another. It was not possible to allow the dress to tear. "I in the thorny bush," she said. "Thorns, you doing your appointed work. Never want to let folks pass, no sir. Old eyes thought you was a pretty little *green* bush."

Finally, trembling all over, she stood free, and after a moment dared to stoop for her cane.

"Sun so high!" she cried, leaning back and looking, while the thick tears went over her eyes. "The time getting all gone here."

At the foot of this hill was a place where a log was laid across the creek.

"Now comes the trial," said Phoenix.

Putting her right foot out, she mounted the log and shut her eyes. Lifting her skirt, leveling her cane fiercely before her, like a festival figure in some parade, she began to march across. Then she opened her eyes and she was safe on the other side.

"I wasn't as old as I thought," she said.

But she sat down to rest. She spread her skirts on the bank around her and folded her hands over her knees. Up above her was a tree in a pearly cloud of mistletoe. She did not dare to close her eyes, and when a little boy brought her a plate with a slice of marble-cake on it she spoke to him. "That would be acceptable," she said. But when she went to take it there was just her own hand in the air.

So she left that tree, and had to go through a barbed-wire fence. There she had to creep and crawl, spreading her knees and stretching her fingers like a baby trying to climb the steps. But she talked loudly to herself: she could not let her dress be torn now, so late in the day, and she could not pay for having her arm or her leg sawed off if she got caught fast where she was.

At last she was safe through the fence and risen up out in the clearing. Big dead trees, like black men with one arm, were standing in the purple stalks of the withered cotton field. There sat a buzzard.

"Who you watching?"

In the furrow she made her way along.

"Glad this not the season for bulls," she said, looking sideways, "and the good Lord made his snakes to curl up and sleep in the winter. A pleasure I don't see no two-headed snake coming around that tree, where it come once. It took a while to get by him, back in the summer."

She passed through the old cotton and went into a field of dead corn. It whispered and shook and was taller than her head. "Through the maze now," she said, for there was no path.

Then there was something tall, black, and skinny there, moving before her.

At first she took it for a man. It could have been a man dancing in the field. But she stood still and listened, and it did not make a sound. It was as silent as a ghost.

"Ghost," she said sharply, "who be you the ghost of? For I have heard of nary death close by."

But there was no answer—only the ragged dancing in the wind.

She shut her eyes, reached out her hand, and touched a sleeve. She found a coat and inside that an emptiness, cold as ice.

"You scarecrow," she said. Her face lighted. "I ought to be shut up for good," she said with laughter. "My senses is gone. I too old. I the oldest people I ever know. Dance, old scarecrow," she said, "while I dancing with you."

She kicked her foot over the furrow, and with mouth drawn down, shook her head once or twice in a little strutting way. Some husks blew down and whirled in streamers about her skirts.

Then she went on, parting her way from side to side with the cane, through the whispering field. At last she came to the end, to a wagon track where the silver grass blew between the red ruts. The quail were walking around like pullets, seeming all dainty and unseen.

"Walk pretty," she said. "This the easy place. This the easy going."

She followed the track, swaying through the quiet bare fields, through the little strings of trees silver in their dead leaves, past cabins silver from weather, with the doors and windows boarded shut, all like old women under a spell sitting there. "I walking in their sleep," she said, nodding her head vigorously.

In a ravine she went where a spring was silently flowing through a hollow log. Old Phoenix bent and drank. "Sweet-gum makes the water sweet," she said, and drank more. "Nobody know who made this well, for it was here when I born."

The track crossed a swampy part where the moss hung as white as lace from every limb. "Sleep on, alligators, and blow your bubbles." Then the track went into the road.

Deep, deep the road went down between the high green-colored banks. Overhead the live-oaks met, and it was as dark as a cave.

A black dog with a lolling tongue came up out of the weeds by the ditch. She was meditating, and not ready and when he came at her she only hit him a little with her cane. Over she went in the ditch, like a little puff of milkweed.

Down there, her senses drifted away. A dream visited her, and she reached her hand up, but nothing reached down and gave her a pull. So she lay there and presently went to talking. "Old woman," she said to herself, "that black dog come up out of the weeds to stall you off, and now here he sitting on his fine tail, smiling at you."

A white man finally came along and found her—a hunter, a young man, with his dog on a chain.

"Well, Granny!" he laughed. "What are you doing there?"

"Lying on my back like a June-bug waiting to be turned over, mister," she said, reaching up her hand.

He lifted her up, gave her a swing in the air, and set her down. "Anything broken, Granny?"

"No sir, them old dead weeds is springy enough," said Phoenix, when she had got her breath. "I thank you for your trouble."

"Where do you live, Granny?" he asked, while the two dogs were growling at each other.

"Away back yonder, sir, behind the ridge. You can't even see it from here."

"On your way home?"

"No sir, I going to town."

"Why, that's too far! That's as far as I walk when I come out myself, and I get something for my trouble." He patted the stuffed bag he carried, and there hung down a little closed claw. It was one of the bob-whites, with its beak hooked bitterly to show it was dead. "Now you go on home, Granny!"

"I bound to go to town, mister," said Phoenix. "The time come around."

He gave another laugh, filling the whole landscape. "I know you old colored people! Wouldn't miss going to town to see Santa Claus!"

But something held old Phoenix very still. The deep lines in her face went into a fierce and different radiation. Without warning, she had seen with her own eyes a flashing nickel fall out of the man's pocket onto the ground.

"How old are you, Granny?" he was saying.

"There is no telling, mister," she said, "no telling."

Then she gave a little cry and clapped her hands and said, "Git on away from here, dog! Look! Look at that dog!" She laughed as if in admiration. "He ain't scared of nobody. He a big black dog." She whispered, "Sic him!"

"Watch me get rid of that cur," said the man, "Sic him, Pete! Sic him!"

Phoenix heard the dogs fighting, and heard the man running and throwing sticks. She even heard a gunshot. But she was slowly bending forward by that time, further and further forward, the lids stretched down over her eyes, as if she were doing this in her sleep. Her chin was lowered almost to her knees. The yellow palm of her hand came out from the fold of her apron. Her fingers slid down and along the ground under the piece of money with the grace and care they would have in lifting an egg from under a setting hen. Then she slowly straightened up, she stood erect, and the nickel was in her apron pocket. A bird flew by. Her lips moved. "God watching me the whole time. I come to stealing."

The man came back, and his own dog panted about them. "Well, I scared him off that time," he said, and then he laughed and lifted his gun and pointed it at Phoenix.

She stood straight and faced him.

"Doesn't the gun scare you?" he said, still pointing it.

"No sir, I seen plenty go off closer by, in my day, and for less than what I done," she said, holding utterly still.

He smiled, and shouldered the gun. "Well, Granny," he said, "you must be a hundred years old, and scared of nothing. I'd give you a dime if I had any money with me. But you take my advice and stay home, and nothing will happen to you."

"I bound to go on my way, mister," said Phoenix. She inclined her head in the red rag. Then they went in different directions, but she could hear the gun shooting again and again over the hill.

She walked on. The shadows hung from the oak trees to the road like curtains. Then she smelled wood-smoke, and smelled the river, and she saw a steeple and the cabins on their steep steps. Dozens of little black children whirled around her. There ahead was Natchez shining. Bells were ringing. She walked on.

In the paved city it was Christmas time. There were red and green electric lights strung and crisscrossed everywhere, and all turned on in the daytime. Old Phoenix would have been lost if she had not distrusted her eyesight and depended on her feet to know where to take her.

She paused quietly on the sidewalk where people were passing by. A lady came along in the crowd, carrying an armful of red-, green- and silver-wrapped presents; she gave off perfume like the red roses in hot summer, and Phoenix stopped her.

"Please, missy, will you lace up my shoe?" She held up her foot.

"What do you want, Grandma?"

"See my shoe," said Phoenix. "Do all right for out in the country, but wouldn't look right to go in a big building."

"Stand still then, Grandma," said the lady. She put her packages down on the sidewalk beside her and laced and tied both shoes tightly.

"Can't lace 'em with a cane," said Phoenix. "Thank you, missy. I doesn't mind asking a nice lady to tie up my shoe, when I gets out on the street."

Moving slowly and from side to side, she went into the big building and into a tower of steps, where she walked up and around and around until her feet knew to stop.

She entered a door, and there she saw nailed up on the wall the document that had been stamped with the gold seal and framed in the gold frame, which matched the dream that was hung up in her head.

"Here I be," she said. There was a fixed and ceremonial stiffness over her body.

"A charity case, I suppose," said an attendant who sat at the desk before her.

But Phoenix only looked above her head. There was sweat on her face, the wrinkles in her skin shone like a bright net.

"Speak up, Grandma," the woman said. "What's your name? We must have your history, you know. Have you been here before? What seems to be the trouble with you?"

Old Phoenix only gave a twitch to her face as if a fly were bothering her.

"Are you deaf?" cried the attendant.

But then the nurse came in.

"Oh, that's just old Aunt Phoenix," she said. "She doesn't come for herself—she has a little grandson. She makes these trips just as regular as clockwork. She lives away back off the Old Natchez Trace." She bent down. "Well, Aunt Phoenix, why don't you just take a seat? We won't keep you standing after your long trip." She pointed.

The old woman sat down, bolt upright in the chair.

"Now, how is the boy?"

Old Phoenix did not speak.

"I said, how is the boy?"

But Phoenix only waited and stared straight ahead, her face very solemn and withdrawn into rigidity.

"Is his throat any better?" asked the nurse. "Aunt Phoenix, don't you hear me? Is your grandson's throat any better since the last time you came for the medicine?"

With her hands on her knees, the old woman waited, silent, erect and motionless, just as if she were in armor.

"You mustn't take up our time this way, Aunt Phoenix," the nurse said. "Tell us quickly about your grandson, and get it over. He isn't dead, is he?"

At last there came a flicker and then a flame of comprehension across her face, and she spoke.

"My grandson. It was my memory had left me. There I sat and forgot why I made my long trip."

"Forgot?" The nurse frowned. "After you came so far?"

Then Phoenix was like an old woman begging a dignified forgiveness for waking up frightened in the night. "I never did go to school, I was too old at the Surrender," she said in a soft voice. "I'm an old woman without an education. It was my memory fail me. My little grandson, he is just the same, and I forgot it in the coming."

"Throat never heals, does it?" said the nurse, speaking in a loud, sure voice to old Phoenix. By now she had a card with something written on it, a little list. "Yes. Swallowed lye. When was it?—January—two, three years ago—"

Phoenix spoke unasked now. "No, missy, he not dead, he just the same. Every little while his throat begin to close up again, and he not able to swallow. He not get his breath. He not able to help himself. So the time come around, and I go on another trip for the soothing medicine."

"All right. The doctor said as long as you came to get it, you could have it," said the nurse. "But it's an obstinate case."

"My little grandson, he sit up there in the house all wrapped up, waiting by himself," Phoenix went on. "We is the only two left in the world. He suffer and it don't seem to put him back at all. He got a sweet look. He going to last. He wear a little patch quilt and peep out holding his mouth open like a little bird. I remembers so plain now. I not going to forget him again, no, the whole enduring time. I could tell him from all the others in creation."

"All right." The nurse was trying to hush her now. She brought her a bottle of medicine. "Charity," she said, making a check mark in a book.

Old Phoenix held the bottle close to her eyes, and then carefully put it into her pocket.

"I thank you," she said.

"It's Christmas time, Grandma," said the attendant. "Could I give you a few pennies out of my purse?"

"Five pennies is a nickel," said Phoenix stiffly.

"Here's a nickel," said the attendant.

Phoenix rose carefully and held out her hand. She received the nickel and then fished the other nickel out of her pocket and laid it beside the new one. She stared at her palm closely, with her head on one side.

Then she gave a tap with her cane on the floor.

"This is what come to me to do," she said. "I going to the store and buy my child a little windmill they sells, made out of paper. He going to find it hard to believe there such a thing in the world. I'll march myself back where he waiting, holding it straight up in this hand."

She lifted her free hand, gave a little nod, turned around, and walked out of the doctor's office. Then her slow step began on the stairs, going down.

Log Entry 5

This log entry has four steps. First, write down your response to the story. Write whatever you think about it.

Then, using the double-entry log format, select and respond to one or more quotations from the story that deal with each of the following:

- the nature of Phoenix's journey, the kinds of obstacles she must overcome, how she deals with them

- Phoenix's character and how it is revealed

- the landscape itself and the contrasts in terrain as she makes her way to the city

- the reason Phoenix keeps going

Next, record and respond to any other parts of the story that you find provocative, puzzling, or interesting.

Finally read the following background information about the meaning of the word *phoenix* and tell how knowing the meaning of Phoenix Jackson's name deepens or enhances your understanding of this story. (If you already know the story of the phoenix, comment on how that knowledge influenced your reading.)

The phoenix is a fabulous Arabian bird, the only one of its kind, that is said to live a certain number of years. At the end of its life it makes, in Arabia, a nest of spices, sings a melodious dirge, flaps its wings to set fire to the nest, burns itself to ashes, and comes forth with new life. It is a symbol of immortality.

Over the years, many students have written to Eudora Welty to ask her about the grandchild in "A Worn Path." Some of them imagined that the child was really dead and that her journey was somehow raised to some new symbolic level because of that interpretation. In responding to these students, Welty deals with some of basic issues about writing fiction—about the relationship of fiction and truth, about words meaning what they say. Here is her response to students who have asked her about the grandchild.

Is Phoenix Jackson's Grandson Really Dead?
Eudora Welty

Reticent, like many writers, when asked to explain her work, Eudora Welty once wrote: "I never saw, as reader or writer, that a finished short story stood in need of any more from the author: for better or worse, there the story is." But because of the many letters she received about Phoenix's grandson, Welty finally decided, in 1974, to respond in the following essay. "Is Phoenix Jackson's Grandson Really Dead?" was then collected with other essays, in 1977, in The Eye of the Story. *In addition to responding to readers' queries, Welty gives us insight into the writer's craft and the values of literature.*

A story writer is more than happy to be read by students; the fact that these serious readers think and feel something in response to his work he finds life-giving. At the same time he may not always be able to reply to their specific questions in kind. I wondered if it might clarify something, for both the questioners and myself, if I set down a general reply to the question that comes to me most often in the mail, from both students and their teachers, after some classroom discussion. The unrivaled favorite is this: "Is Phoenix Jackson's grandson really *dead?*"

It refers to a short story I wrote years ago called "A Worn Path," which tells of a day's journey an old woman makes on foot from deep in the country into town and into a doctor's office on behalf of her little grandson; he is at home, periodically ill, and periodically she comes for his medicine; they give it to her as usual, she receives it and starts the journey back.

I had not meant to mystify readers by withholding any fact; it is not a writer's business to tease. The story is told through Phoenix's mind as she undertakes her errand. As the author at one with the character as I tell it, I must assume that the boy is alive. As the reader, you are free to think as you like, of course: the story invites you to believe that no matter what happens, Phoenix for as long as she is able to walk and can hold to her purpose will make her journey. The *possibility* that she would keep on even if he were dead is there in her devotion and its single-minded, single-track errand. Certainly the *artistic* truth, which should be good enough for the fact, lies in Phoenix's own answer to that question. When the nurse asks, "He isn't dead, is he?" she speaks for herself: "He still the same. He going to last."

The grandchild is the incentive. But it is the journey, the going of the errand, that is the story, and the question is not whether the grandchild is in reality alive or dead. It doesn't affect the outcome of the story or its meaning from start to finish. But it is not the question itself that has struck me as much as the idea, almost without exception implied in the asking, that for Phoenix's grandson to be dead would somehow make the story "better."

It's all right, I want to say to the students who write to me, for things to be what they appear to be, and for words to mean what they say. It's all right, too, for words and appearances to mean more than one thing—ambiguity is a fact of life. A fiction writer's responsibility covers not only what he presents as the facts of a given story but what he chooses to stir up as their implications; in the end, these implications, too, become facts, in the larger, fictional sense. But it is not all right, not in good faith, for things *not* to mean what they say.

The grandson's plight was real and it made the truth of the story, which is the story of an errand of love carried out. If the child no longer lived, the truth would persist in the "wornness" of the path.

But his being dead can't increase the truth of the story, can't affect it one way or the other. I think I signal this, because the end of the story has been reached before old Phoenix gets home again: she simply starts back. To the question "Is the grandson really dead?" I could reply that it doesn't make any difference. I could also say that I did not make him up in order to let him play a trick on Phoenix. But my best answer would be: *"Phoenix is alive."*

The origin of a story is sometimes a trustworthy clue to the author—or can provide him with the clue—to its key image; maybe in this case it will do the same for the reader. One day I saw a solitary old woman like Phoenix. She was walking; I saw her, at middle distance, in a winter country landscape, and watched her slowly make her way across my line of vision. That sight of her made me write the story. I invented an errand for her, but that only seemed a living part of the figure she was herself: what errand other than for someone else could be making her go? And her going was the first thing, her persisting in her landscape was the real thing, and the first and the real were what I wanted and worked to keep. I brought her up close enough, by imagination, to describe her face, make her present to the eyes, but the full-length figure moving across the winter fields was the indelible one and the image to keep, and the perspective extending into the vanishing distance the true one to hold in mind.

I invented for my character, as I wrote, some passing adventures—some dreams and harassments and a small triumph or two, some jolts to her pride, some flights of fancy to console her, one or two encounters to scare her, a moment that gave her cause to feel ashamed, a moment to dance and preen—for it had to be a *journey,* and all these things belonged to that, parts of life's uncertainty.

A narrative line is in its deeper sense, of course, the tracing out of a meaning, and the real continuity of a story lies in this probing forward. The real dramatic force of a story depends on the strength of the emotion that has set it going. The emotional value is the measure of the reach of the story. What gives any such content to "A Worn Path" is not its circumstances but its *subject:* the deep-grained habit of love.

What I hoped would come clear was that in the whole surround of this story, the world it threads through, the only certain thing at all is the worn path. The habit of love cuts through confusion and stumbles or contrives its way out of difficulty, it remembers the way even when it forgets, for a dumbfounded moment, its reason for being. The path is the thing that matters.

Her victory—old Phoenix's—is when she sees the diploma in the doctor's office, when she finds "nailed up on the wall the document that had been stamped with the gold seal and framed in the gold frame, which matched the dream that was hung up in her head." The return with the medicine is just a matter of retracing her own footsteps. It is the part of the journey, and of the story, that can now go without saying.

In the matter of function, old Phoenix's way might even do as a sort of parallel to your way of work if you are a writer of stories. The way to get there is the all-important, all-absorbing problem, and this problem is your reason for undertaking the story. Your only guide, too, is your sureness about your subject, about what this subject is. Like Phoenix, you work all your life to find your way, through all the obstructions and the false appearances and the up- sets you may have brought on yourself, to reach a meaning—using inventions of your imagination, perhaps helped out by your dreams and bits of good luck. And finally too, like Phoenix, you have to as- sume that what you are working in aid of is life, not death.

But you would make the trip anyway—wouldn't you—just on hope.

Collaborating

Talk about Welty's response to students. Explore your own ideas and reactions to her comments.

Log Entry 6

Write responses to passages from the essay that deal with some of the issues Welty discusses in her response to students. Use the fol- lowing quotations or any others that helped you understand this story, the function of a writer, or the relationship between truth and fiction.

"As a reader, you are free to think as you like, of course."

"Certainly the artistic truth . . . lies in Phoenix's own answer to that question."

"But it is the journey, the going of the errand, that is the story . . ."

"The real dramatic force of a story depends on the strength of the emotion that has set it going."

*W*ork in Progress

Select one or more of these suggestions to include in your writing folder:

Graphic and written journeys

- With one or two classmates, create a graphic representation of Phoenix Jackson's journey. Include references to other pieces of literature, television shows, or movies that deal with the idea of a person's journey.

- Write a research paper or reflective essay about journeys in literature, television shows, or movies.

Journeys from nonfiction to fiction

- Think about some phase of your life that could be described in terms of a journey. Map it graphically; then write about it.

- Using some seed or germ of an idea from your own journey or your own observations, create a short story about a journey taken by a fictional character.

- Write a reflective essay on this quotation from Welty's response to students: "*It's all right,* I want to say to the students who write to me, for things to be what they appear to be, and for words to mean what they say. It's all right, too, for words and appearances to mean more than one thing—ambiguity is a fact of life."

*T*ruth in Fiction and Nonfiction, Life and Art

Think again about the question of nonfiction and fiction, true and false, real and made up. Reread this section of the story "Starting Out," which begins with Phil asking the writer/doctor a question.

> "Have you ever read a book that really made a difference to you—a book you couldn't get out of your mind, and you didn't want to [get it out of your mind]?"
>
> "Yes, I said". . . We got into a long talk about Dr. Williams's medical work with mostly poor and working-class people, about his effort through stories and poems to understand America's social history and moral values.
>
> . . . I will never forget the direction of our discussion afterward. Phil wondered whether Williams would ever have been able to accomplish what he did, were he not inspired by what he saw all the time as a practicing physician. Then he wondered whether Mark Twain, whose life he had briefly studied, would have been able to do the kind of writing *he* did, had he not been such an inveterate wanderer before he found himself having much to say. The reason for Phil's interest in pointing out the connection between art and life was not too hard for me to comprehend—or for him, either.

*L*og Entry 7

Reflect on the following ideas in your log.

- The connection between art and life is related to the connection between fiction and nonfiction. Do the distinctions begin to blur?

- How much of a writer's life is incorporated into the fictions that he or she creates?

- Is nonfiction any truer than fiction?

The Dr. Williams that Robert Coles refers to as he talks with Phil about books that had made a difference in his life is the poet/doctor William Carlos Williams. Although he was a lifelong doctor, a gen-

eral practitioner who made house calls, he was one of the most influential poets of his time. In addition to his many books of poems,
he wrote a short autobiography called *I Wanted to Write a Poem:
The Autobiography of the Works of a Poet*. In this book, Williams
talks about how books came to be important to him. Compare his
experience with that of Phil, who was about the same age as
Williams when he discovered his first important book. Was
Williams born a poet? In this excerpt he answers that question.

I Wanted to Write a Poem: The Autobiography
of the Works of a Poet
William Carlos Williams

Was he a born poet, wanting to write as far back as he could remember?

No, no. It began with a heart attack. I was sixteen or seventeen.
There was a race. Mismanaged. I ran the eight laps. Someone
called, "You've got another lap to run." I ran it. I was sick, vomiting
sick, and my head hurt. When I got home my family called old Doc
Calhoun. He said, "Heart murmur." Oh, I don't know, I may have
had rheumatic fever without knowing it. Anyhow, it meant a complete change in my life. I had lived for sports like any other kid.
They let me go to school. But no more baseball. No more running. I
didn't mind the running too much . . . there was a boy up the street
I never could beat. But the rest. Not being with the others after
school. I was forced back on myself. I had to think about myself,
look into myself. And I began to read.

In Uncle Billy Abbott's class at Horace Mann we read a book of
Robert Louis Stevenson's—a travel book I think it was. There was a
young man and an upset canoe and a line that said, "I never let go
of that paddle." I was crazy about that line. I'd say it over and over
to myself. I wrote a theme about it and Uncle Billy Abbott gave me
an A−. The best mark I'd ever had. I was thrilled.

(The book referred to was *An Inland Voyage* and the line appears
at the end of the chapter, "The Oise in Flood." Stevenson also appears to have been "crazy about that line"—he repeats it four times:
"I still clung to my paddle." "And I still held to my paddle." "But
there was my paddle in my hand." And finally, "On my tomb, if ever
I have one, I mean to get these words inscribed: 'He clung to his
paddle.'")

I don't remember learning any nursery rhymes, but I do remember my grandmother teaching me my prayer. It was:

Gentle Jesus, meek and mild,
Look upon a little child
Pity my simplicity . . .

—and the rest of it. I can still say it word for word. But at one point I refused to say it every night. I must have been very little. I didn't see why I had to say it every night. I'd say, "I'm not going to say it tonight"—lying, looking up at the ceiling, expecting to be struck dead.

My father was an Englishman who never got over being an Englishman. He had a love of the written word. Shakespeare meant everything to him. He read the plays to mother and my brother and myself. He read well. I was deeply impressed. He read Negro dialect poems, too; simple poetry but it had swing and rhythm and quiet humor. I remember one poem, "Accountability." Paul Lawrence Dunbar wrote it. "Put on de kettle . . . I got one of mastah's chickens"—something like that. And Pop read passages from the Bible, over and over. Isaiah was my favorite. I was not influenced by the New Testament. I thought the most impressive thing in the church service was the doxology: "The Peace of God which passeth all understanding"—I used to feel that peace when I heard that line. Yet I wasn't really religious. I went to church to hear the readings and the music. But I'm afraid I *was* rather a sanctimonious young man.

My brother Ed who was later to become a distinguished architect was my first intimate. He was a year younger and bigger almost from the start. We grew up cheek and jowl together. It was nip and tuck with us when we found my mother's discarded oil colors in the attic, the old tubes half squeezed out. I remember the cobalt, smaller than the other tubes because it was expensive, and the palette showing heavy use. I might easily have become a painter and in some ways I regret that I did not go on with it except that the articulate art of poetry gave a more immediate opportunity for the attack.

At first, not even my brother knew about my new world of books. I didn't talk about it to anyone. My discovery of poetry began with the classics we read at school: "Il Penseroso," "L'Allegro," "Lycidas," *Comus*, "The Ancient Mariner." My, but I was excited. But my friends were my former baseball pals. They wouldn't have understood. So it was entirely my own for a long time. And I can't remember consciously thinking at this stage that I wanted to be a poet.

The first line I ever wrote came out of the blue, with no past.

A black, black cloud
flew over the sun
driven by fierce flying
rain.

The thrill. The discovery. At once, at the same instant, I said to myself, "Ridiculous, the rain can't drive the clouds." So the critical thing was being born at the same time.

And now my brother was my confessor. I wrote him poems and sent him poems. He was at Massachusetts Institute of Technology studying architecture and I was at the University of Pennsylvania studying medicine. Ed spoke to Arlo Bates, his English professor, about me and arranged a meeting. It was the weekend of the Harvard-Penn game (which by the way Penn won and I remember I guessed the exact score in a pool and won the money). This was my Keats period. Everything I wrote was bad Keats. I arrived at Mr. Bates's house with my *Endymion* imitation, a big bulky manuscript I'd been slaving over; I don't even remember the name of it. A butler let me in Mr. Bates's bachelor apartment. He was sitting at a desk, the picture of a distinguished man. There was a step down and I tripped and dropped the manuscript. It rolled all over the floor. Mr. Bates was kind. He perused the sonnets and said, "I see you have been reading Keats." "I don't read anything else but him," I said. He said, "Well, you certainly have paid attention to how the sonnet is constructed. I'll tell you a little story. I myself write poems. When I've finished them to my satisfaction I place them in this drawer and there they remain. You may, I can't tell, develop into a writer, but you have a lot to learn. Maybe in time you'll write some good verse. Go on writing, but don't give up medicine. Writing alone is not an easy occupation for a man to follow." This was a turning point in my life. I didn't give up medicine but there was never a minute's thought of giving up writing.

Collaborating

Talk about the similarities and differences between Williams's and Phil's experiences as they came to understand the value of books in their lives. Try to tie their experiences to any that you may have had.

Log Entry 8

Write a reflective log entry on what truth means to you—in life and in art, in nonfiction and fiction.

From Newspaper to Short Story

Though Stephen Crane had not witnessed a single battle before he wrote *The Red Badge of Courage* in 1895, the immense popularity of the novel helped establish a career for him as a leading war correspondent. Crane spent most of his remaining years traveling, despite ill health, to cover the Greco-Turkish, the Boer, and the Spanish-American wars.

"Stephen Crane's Own Story" details his experiences during the wreck of the Commodore, a cargo ship carrying guns and ammunition to Cuban insurgents. His account of this event, as it appeared in the *New York Press* on January 7, 1897, follows. Note that he uses the word *filibusters* not to refer to the long-winded speeches made by congressmen, but to "an irregular military adventurer or buccaneer," the original meaning of the word.

Stephen Crane's Own Story
[He Tells How the Commodore Was Wrecked and How He Escaped]
Stephen Crane

JACKSONVILLE, FLA., Jan. 6.—It was the afternoon of New Year's. The Commodore lay at her dock in Jacksonville and Negro stevedores processioned steadily toward her with box after box of ammunition and bundle after bundle of rifles. Her hatch, like the mouth of a monster, engulfed them. It might have been the feeding time of some legendary creature of the sea. It was in broad daylight and the crowd of gleeful Cubans on the pier did not forbear to sing the strange patriotic ballads of their island.

Everything was perfectly open. The Commodore was cleared with a cargo of arms and munition for Cuba. There was none of that extreme modesty about the proceeding which had marked previous departures of the famous tug. She loaded up as placidly as if she were going to carry oranges to New York, instead of Remingtons to Cuba. Down the river, furthermore, the revenue cutter Boutwell, the old isosceles triangle that protects United States interests in the St. John's, lay at anchor, with no sign of excitement aboard her.

Exchanging Farewells

On the decks of the Commodore there were exchanges of farewells in two languages. Many of the men who were to sail upon her had many intimates in the old Southern town, and we who had left our friends in the remote North received our first touch of melancholy on witnessing these strenuous and earnest goodbys.

It seems, however, that there was more difficulty at the custom house. The officers of the ship and the Cuban leaders were detained there until a mournful twilight settled upon the St. John's, and through a heavy fog the lights of Jacksonville blinked dimly. Then at last the Commodore swung clear of the dock, amid a tumult of goodbys. As she turned her bow toward the distant sea the Cubans ashore cheered and cheered. In response the Commodore gave three long blasts of her whistle, which even to this time impressed me with their sadness. Somehow, they sounded as wails.

Then at last we began to feel like filibusters. I don't suppose that the most stolid brain could contrive to believe that there is not a mere trifle of danger in filibustering, and so as we watched the lights of Jacksonville swing past us and heard the regular thump, thump, thump of the engines we did considerable reflecting.

But I am sure that there were no hifalutin emotions visible upon any of the faces which fronted the speeding shore. In fact, from cook's boy to captain, we were all enveloped in a gentle satisfaction and cheerfulness. But less than two miles from Jacksonville, this atrocious fog caused the pilot to ram the bow of the Commodore hard upon the mud and in this ignominious position we were compelled to stay until daybreak.

Help from the Boutwell

It was to all of us more than a physical calamity. We were now no longer filibusters. We were men on a ship stuck in the mud. A certain mental somersault was made once more necessary.

But word had been sent to Jacksonville to the captain of the revenue cutter Boutwell, and Captain Kilgore turned out promptly and generously fired up his old triangle, and came at full speed to our assistance. She dragged us out of the mud, and again we headed for the mouth of the river. The revenue cutter pounded along a half mile astern of us, to make sure that we did not take on board at some place along the river men for the Cuban army.

This was the early morning of New Year's Day, and the fine golden southern sunlight fell full upon the river. It flashed over the ancient Boutwell, until her white sides gleamed like pearl, and her rigging was spun into little threads of gold.

Cheers greeted the old Commodore from passing ship and from the shore. It was a cheerful, almost merry, beginning to our voyage. At Mayport, however, we changed our river pilot for a man who could take her to open sea, and again the Commodore was beached. The Boutwell was fussing around us in her venerable way, and, upon seeing our predicament, she came again to assist us, but this time, with engines reversed, the Commodore dragged herself away from the grip of the sand and again headed for the open sea.

The captain of the revenue cutter grew curious. He hailed the Commodore: "Are you fellows going to sea to-day?"

Captain Murphy of the Commodore called back: "Yes, sir."

And then as the whistle of the Commodore saluted him, Captain Kilgore doffed his cap and said: "Well, gentlemen, I hope you have a pleasant cruise," and this was our last word from shore.

When the Commodore came to enormous rollers that flew over the bar a certain light-heartedness departed from the ship's company.

Sleep Impossible

As darkness came upon the waters, the Commodore was a broad, flaming path of blue and silver phosphorescence, and as her stout bow lunged at the great black waves she threw flashing, roaring cascades to either side. And all that was to be heard was rhythmical and mighty pounding of the engines. Being an inexperienced fili-buster, the writer had undergone considerable mental excitement since the starting of the ship, and in consequence he had not yet been to sleep and so I went to the first mate's bunk to indulge my-self in all the physical delights of holding oneself in bed. Every time the ship lurched I expected to be fired through a bulkhead, and it was neither amusing nor instructive to see in the dim light a certain accursed valise aiming itself at the top of my stomach with every lurch of the vessel.

The Cook Is Hopeful

The cook was asleep on a bench in the galley. He is of a portly and noble exterior, and by means of a checker board he had himself wedged on this bench in such a manner the motion of the ship would be unable to dislodge him. He woke as I entered the galley and delivered himself of some dolorous sentiments: "God," he said in the course of his observations, "I don't feel right about this ship, somehow. It strikes me that something is going to happen to us. I don't know what it is, but the old ship is going to get it in the neck, I think."

"Well, how about the men on board her?" said I. "Are any of us going to get out, prophet?"

"Yes," said the cook. "Sometimes I have these damned feelings come over me, and they are always right, and it seems to me, somehow, that you and I will both get out and meet again somewhere, down at Coney Island, perhaps, or some place like that."

One Man Has Enough

Finding it impossible to sleep, I went back to the pilot house. An old seaman, Tom Smith, from Charleston, was then at the wheel. In the darkness I could not see Tom's face, except at those times when he leaned forward to scan the compass and the dim light from the box came upon his weatherbeaten features.

"Well, Tom," said I, "how do you like filibustering?"

He said "I think I am about through with it. I've been in a number of these expeditions and the pay is good, but I think if I ever get back safe this time I will cut it."

I sat down in the corner of the pilot house and almost went to sleep. In the meantime the captain came on duty and he was standing near me when the chief engineer rushed up the stairs and cried hurriedly to the captain that there was something wrong in the engine room. He and the captain departed swiftly.

I was drowsing there in my corner when the captain returned, and, going to the door of the little room directly back of the pilot house, he cried to the Cuban leader: "Say, can't you get those fellows to work. I can't talk their language and I can't get them started. Come on and get them going."

Helps in the Fireroom

The Cuban leader turned to me and said: "Go help in the fireroom. They are going to bail with buckets."

The engine room, by the way, represented a scene at this time taken from the middle kitchen of Hades. In the first place, it was insufferably warm, and the lights burned faintly in a way to cause mystic and gruesome shadows. There was a quantity of soapish sea water swirling and sweeping and swishing among machinery that roared and banged and clattered and steamed, and, in the second place, it was a devil of a ways down below.

Here I first came to know a certain young oiler named Billy Higgins. He was sloshing around this inferno filling buckets with water and passing them to a chain of men that extended up the ship's side. Afterward we got orders to change our point of attack on water and to operate through a little door on the windward side of the ship that led into the engine room.

No Panic on Board

During this time there was much talk of pumps out of order and many other statements of a mechanical kind, which I did not altogether comprehend but understood to mean that there was a general and sudden ruin in the engine room.

There was no particular agitation at this time, and even later there was never a panic on board the Commodore. The party of men who worked with Higgins and me at this time were all Cubans, and we were under the direction of the Cuban leaders. Presently we were ordered again to the afterhold, and there was some hesitation about going into the abominable fireroom again, but Higgins dashed down the companion way with a bucket.

Lowering Boats

The heat and hard work in the fireroom affected me and I was obliged to come on deck again. Going forward, I heard as I went talk of lowering the boats. Near the corner of the galley the mate was talking with a man.

"Why don't you send up a rocket?" said this unknown man. And the mate replied: "What the hell do we want to send up a rocket for? The ship is all right."

Returning with a little rubber and cloth overcoat, I saw the first boat about to be lowered. A certain man was the first person in this first boat, and they were handing him in a valise about as large as a hotel. I had not entirely recovered from astonishment and pleasure in witnessing this noble deed when I saw another valise go to him.

Human Hog Appears

This valise was not perhaps so large as a hotel, but it was a big valise anyhow. Afterward there went to him something which looked to me like an overcoat.

Seeing the chief engineer leaning out of his little window, I remarked to him:

"What do you think of that blank, blank, blank?"

"Oh, he's a bird," said the old chief.

It was now that was heard the order to get away the lifeboat, which was stowed on top of the deckhouse. The deckhouse was a mighty slippery place, and with each roll of the ship, the men there thought themselves likely to take headers into the deadly black sea.

Higgins was on top of the deckhouse, and, with the first mate and two colored stokers, we wrestled with that boat, which, I am willing to swear, weighed as much as a Broadway cable car. She might have been spiked to the deck. We could have pushed a little brick schoolhouse along a corduroy road as easily as we could have moved this boat. But the first mate got a tackle to her from a leeward davit, and on the deck below the captain corralled enough men to make an impression upon the boat.

We were ordered to cease hauling then, and in this lull the cook of the ship came to me and said: "What are you going to do?"

I told him of my plans, and he said: "Well, my God, that's what I am going to do."

A Whistle of Despair

Now the whistle of the Commodore had been turned loose, and if there ever was a voice of despair and death, it was in the voice of this whistle. It had gained a new tone. It was as if its throat was already choked by the water, and this cry on the sea at night, with a wind blowing the spray over the ship, and the waves roaring over the bow, and swirling white along the decks, was to each of us probably a song of man's end.

It was now that the first mate showed a sign of losing his grip. To us who were trying in all stages of competence and experience to launch the lifeboat he raged in all terms of fiery satire and hammerlike abuse. But the boat moved at last and swung down toward the water.

Afterward, when I went aft, I saw the captain standing, with his arm in a sling, holding on to a stay with his one good hand and directing the launching of the boat. He gave me a five-gallon jug of water to hold, and asked me what I was going to do. I told him what I thought was about the proper thing, and he told me then that the cook had the same idea, and ordered me to go forward and be ready to launch the ten-foot dinghy.

In the Ten-Foot Dinghy

I remember well that he turned then to swear at a colored stoker who was prowling around, done up in life preservers until he looked like a feather bed. I went forward with my five-gallon jug of water, and when the captain came we launched the dinghy, and they put me over the side to fend her off from the ship with an oar.

They handed me down the water jug, and then the cook came into the boat, and we sat there in the darkness, wondering why, by all our hopes of future happiness, the captain was so long in coming over to the side and ordering us away from the doomed ship.

The captain was waiting for the other boat to go. Finally he hailed in the darkness: "Are you all right, Mr. Graines?"

The first mate answered: "All right, sir."

"Shove off, then," cried the captain.

The captain was just about to swing over the rail when a dark form came forward and a voice said: "Captain, I go with you."

The captain answered: "Yes, Billy; get in."

Higgins Last to Leave Ship

It was Billy Higgins, the oiler. Billy dropped into the boat and a moment later the captain followed, bringing with him an end of about forty yards of lead line. The other end was attached to the rail of the ship.

As we swung back to leeward the captain said: "Boys, we will stay right near the ship till she goes down."

This cheerful information, of course, filled us all with glee. The line kept us headed properly into the wind, and as we rode over the monstrous waves we saw upon each rise the swaying lights of the dying Commodore.

When came the gray shade of dawn, the form of the Commodore grew slowly clear to us as our little ten-foot boat rose over each swell. She was floating with such an air of buoyancy that we laughed when we had time, and said: "What a gag it would be on those other fellows if she didn't sink at all."

But later we saw men aboard of her, and later still they began to hail us.

Helping Their Mates

I had forgot to mention that previously we had loosened the end of the lead line and dropped much further to leeward. The men on board were a mystery to us, of course, as we had seen all the boats leave the ship. We rowed back to the ship, but did not approach too near, because we were four men in a ten-foot boat, and we knew that the touch of a hand on our gunwale would assuredly swamp us.

The first mate cried out from the ship that the third boat had foundered alongside. He cried that they had made rafts, and wished us to tow them.

The captain said, "All right."

Their rafts were floating astern. "Jump in!" cried the captain, but there was a singular and most harrowing hesitation. There were five white men and two Negroes. This scene in the gray light of morning impressed one as would a view into some place where ghosts move slowly. These seven men on the stern of the sinking Commodore were silent. Save the words of the mate to the captain there was no talk. Here was death, but here also was a most singular and indefinable kind of fortitude.

Four men, I remember, clambered over the railing and stood there watching the cold, steely sheen of the sweeping waves.

"Jump," cried the captain again.

The old chief engineer first obeyed the order. He landed on the outside raft and the captain told him how to grip the raft and he obeyed as promptly and as docilely as a scholar in riding school.

The Mate's Mad Plunge

A stoker followed him, and then the first mate threw his hands over his head and plunged into the sea. He had no life belt and for my part, even when he did this horrible thing, I somehow felt that I could see in the expression of his hands, and in the very toss of his head, as he leaped thus to death, that it was rage, rage, rage unspeakable that was in his heart at the time.

And then I saw Tom Smith, the man who was going to quit filibustering after this expedition, jump to a raft and turn his face toward us. On board the Commodore three men strode, still in silence and with their faces turned toward us. One man had his arms folded and was leaning against the deckhouse. His feet were crossed, so that the toe of his left foot pointed downward. There they stood gazing at us, and neither from the deck nor from the rafts was a voice raised. Still was there this silence.

Tried to Tow the Rafts

The colored stoker on the first raft threw us a line and we began to tow. Of course, we perfectly understood the absolute impossibility of any such thing; our dingy was within six inches of the water's edge, there was an enormous sea running, and I knew that under the circumstances a tugboat would have no light task in moving these rafts.

But we tried it, and would have continued to try it indefinitely, but that something critical came to pass. I was at an oar and so faced the rafts. The cook controlled the line. Suddenly the boat began to go backward and then we saw this Negro on the first raft pulling on the line hand over hand and drawing us to him.

He had turned into a demon. He was wild—wild as a tiger. He was crouched on this raft and ready to spring. Every muscle of him seemed to be turned into an elastic spring. His eyes were almost white. His face was the face of a lost man reaching upward, and we knew that the weight of his hand on our gunwale doomed us.

The Commodore Sinks

The cook let go of the line. We rowed around to see if we could not get a line from the chief engineer, and all this time, mind you, there were no shrieks, no groans, but silence, silence and silence, and then the Commodore sank.

She lurched to windward, then swung afar back, righted and dove into the sea, and the rafts were suddenly swallowed by this frightful maw of the ocean. And then by the men on the ten-foot dingy were words said that were still not words—something far beyond words.

The lighthouse of Mosquito Inlet stuck up above the horizon like the point of a pin. We turned our dingy toward the shore.

The history of life in an open boat for thirty hours would no doubt be instructive for the young, but none is to be told here and now. For my part I would prefer to tell the story at once, because from it would shine the splendid manhood of Captain Edward Mur-

A singular disadvantage of the sea lies in the fact that after successfully surmounting one wave you discover that there is another behind it just as important and just as nervously anxious to do something effective in the way of swamping boats. In a ten-foot dinghy one can get an idea of the resources of the sea in the line of waves that is not probable to the average experience which is never at sea in a dinghy. As each slaty wall of water approached, it shut all else from the view of the men in the boat, and it was not difficult to imagine that this particular wave was the final outburst of the ocean, the last effort of the grim water. There was a terrible grace in the move of the waves, and they came in silence, save for the snarling of the crests.

In the wan light the faces of the men must have been grey. Their eyes must have glinted in strange ways as they gazed steadily astern. Viewed from a balcony, the whole thing would doubtless have been weirdly picturesque. But the men in the boat had no time to see it, and if they had had leisure, there were other things to occupy their minds. The sun swung steadily up the sky, and they knew it was broad day because the colour of the sea changed from slate to emerald green streaked with amber lights, and the foam was like tumbling snow. The process of the breaking day was unknown to them. They were aware only of this effect upon the colour of the waves that rolled toward them.

In disjointed sentences the cook and the correspondent argued as to the difference between a life-saving station and a house of refuge. The cook had said: "There's a house of refuge just north of the Mosquito Inlet Light, and as soon as they see us they'll come off in their boat and pick us up."

"As soon as who see us?" said the correspondent.

"The crew," said the cook.

"Houses of refuge don't have crews," said the correspondent. "As I understand them, they are only places where clothes and grub are stored for the benefit of shipwrecked people. They don't carry crews."

"Oh, yes, they do," said the cook.

"No, they don't," said the correspondent.

"Well, we're not there yet, anyhow," said the oiler, in the stern.

"Well," said the cook, "perhaps it's not a house of refuge that I'm thinking of as being near Mosquito Inlet Light; perhaps it's a life-saving station."

"We're not there yet," said the oiler in the stern.

II

As the boat bounced from the top of each wave the wind tore through the hair of the hatless men, and as the craft plopped her stern down again the spray slashed past them. The crest of each of these waves was a hill, from the top of which the men surveyed for a moment a broad tumultuous expanse, shining and wind-riven. It was probably splendid, it was probably glorious, this play of the free sea, wild with lights of emerald and white and amber.

"Bully good thing it's an on-shore wind," said the cook. "If not, where would we be? Wouldn't have a show."

"That's right," said the correspondent.

The busy oiler nodded his assent.

Then the captain, in the bow, chuckled in a way that expressed humour, contempt, tragedy, all in one. "Do you think we've got much of a show now, boys?" said he.

Whereupon the three were silent, save for a trifle of hemming and hawing. To express any particular optimism at this time they felt to be childish and stupid, but they all doubtless possessed this sense of the situation in their minds. A young man thinks doggedly at such times. On the other hand, the ethics of their condition was decidedly against any open suggestion of hopelessness. So they were silent.

"Oh, well," said the captain, soothing his children, "we'll get ashore all right."

But there was that in his tone which made them think; so the oiler quoth, "Yes! if this wind holds."

The cook was bailing. "Yes! if we don't catch hell in the surf."

Canton-flannel gulls flew near and far. Sometimes they sat down on the sea, near patches of brown seaweed that rolled over the waves with a movement like carpets on a line in a gale. The birds sat comfortably in groups, and they were envied by some in the dinghy, for the wrath of the sea was no more to them than it was to a covey of prairie chickens a thousand miles inland. Often they came very close and stared at the men with black bead-like eyes. At these times they were uncanny and sinister in their unblinking scrutiny, and the men hooted angrily at them, telling them to be gone. One came, and evidently decided to alight on the top of the captain's head. The bird flew parallel to the boat and did not circle, but made short sidelong jumps in the air in chicken-fashion. His black eyes were wistfully fixed upon the captain's head. "Ugly brute," said the oiler to the bird. "You look as if you were made with a jackknife." The cook and the correspondent swore darkly at the creature. The captain naturally wished to knock it away with the end of the heavy painter, but he did not dare do it, because anything resembling an emphatic gesture would have capsized this freighted boat; and so, with his open hand, the captain gently and carefully waved the gull away. After it had been discouraged from the pursuit the captain breathed easier on account of his hair, and others breathed easier because the bird struck their minds at this time as being somehow gruesome and ominous.

In the meantime the oiler and the correspondent rowed. And also they rowed. They sat together in the same seat, and each rowed an oar. Then the oiler took both oars; then the correspondent took both oars; then the oiler; then the correspondent. They rowed and they rowed. The very ticklish part of the business was when the time came for the reclining one in the stern to take his turn at the oars. By the very last star of truth, it is easier to steal eggs from under a hen than it was to change seats in the dinghy. First the man in the stern slid his hand along the thwart and moved with care, as if he were of Sevres. Then the man in the rowing-seat slid his hand along the other thwart. It was all done with the most extraordinary care. As the two sidled past each other, the whole party kept watchful eyes on the coming wave, and the captain cried: "Look out, now! Steady, there!"

The brown mats of seaweed that appeared from time to time were like islands, bits of earth. They were travelling, apparently, neither one way nor the other. They were, to all intents, stationary. They informed the men in the boat that it was making progress slowly toward the land.

The captain, rearing cautiously in the bow after the dinghy soared on a great swell, said that he had seen the lighthouse at Mosquito Inlet. Presently the cook remarked that he had seen it. The correspondent was at the oars then, and for some reason he too wished to look at the lighthouse; but his back was toward the far shore, and the waves were important, and for some time he could not seize an opportunity to turn his head. But at last there came a wave more gentle than the others, and when at the crest of it he swiftly scoured the western horizon.

"See it?" said the captain.

"No," said the correspondent, slowly, "I didn't see anything."

"Look again," said the captain. He pointed. "It's exactly in that direction."

At the top of another wave the correspondent did as he was bid, and this time his eyes chanced on a small, still thing on the edge of the swaying horizon. It was precisely like the point of a pin. It took an anxious eye to find a lighthouse so tiny.

"Think we'll make it, Captain?"

"If this wind holds and the boat don't swamp, we can't do much else," said the captain.

The little boat, lifted by each towering sea and splashed viciously by the crests, made progress that in the absence of seaweed was not apparent to those in her. She seemed just a wee thing wallowing, miraculously top up, at the mercy of five oceans. Occasionally a great spread of water, like white flames, swarmed into her.

"Bail her, Cook," said the captain, serenely.

"All right, Captain," said the cheerful cook.

III

It would be difficult to describe the subtle brotherhood of men that was here established on the seas. No one said that it was so. No one mentioned it. But it dwelt in the boat, and each man felt it warm him. They were a captain, an oiler, a cook, and a correspondent, and they were friends—friends in a more curiously iron-bound degree than may be common. The hurt captain, lying against the water-jar in the bow, spoke always in a low voice and calmly; but he could never command a more ready and swiftly obedient crew than the motley three of the dinghy. It was more than a mere recognition of what was best for common safety. There was surely in it a quality that was personal and heart-felt. And after this devotion to the commander of the boat, there was this comradeship, that the correspondent, for instance, who had been taught to be cynical of men, knew even at the time was the best experience of his life. But no one said that it was so. No one mentioned it.

"I wish we had a sail," remarked the captain. "We might try my overcoat on the end of an oar, and give you two boys a chance to rest." So the cook and the correspondent held the mast and spread wide the overcoat; the oiler steered; and the little boat made good way with her new rig. Sometimes the oiler had to scull sharply to keep a sea from breaking into the boat, but otherwise sailing was a success.

Meanwhile the lighthouse had been growing slowly larger. It had now almost assumed colour, and appeared like a little grey shadow on the sky. The man at the oars could not be prevented from turning his head rather often to try for a glimpse of this little grey shadow.

At last, from the top of each wave, the men in the tossing boat could see land. Even as the lighthouse was an upright shadow on the sky, this land seemed but a long black shadow on the sea. It certainly was thinner than paper. "We must be about opposite New Smyrna," said the cook, who had coasted this shore often in schooners. "Captain, by the way, I believe they abandoned that life-saving station there about a year ago."

"Did they?" said the captain.

The wind slowly died away. The cook and the correspondent were not now obliged to slave in order to hold high the oar. But the waves continued their old impetuous swooping at the dinghy, and the little craft, no longer under way, struggled woundily over them. The oiler or the correspondent took the oars again.

Shipwrecks are apropos of nothing. If men could only train for them and have them occur when the men had reached pink condition, there would be less drowning at sea. Of the four in the dinghy none had slept any time worth mentioning for two days and two nights previous to embarking in the dinghy, and in the excitement of clambering about the deck of a foundering ship they had also forgotten to eat heartily.

For these reasons, and for others, neither the oiler nor the correspondent was fond of rowing at this time. The correspondent wondered ingenuously how in the name of all that was sane could there be people who thought it amusing to row a boat. It was not an amusement; it was a diabolical punishment, and even a genius of mental aberrations could never conclude that it was anything but a horror to the muscles and a crime against the back. He mentioned to the boat in general how the amusement of rowing struck him, and the weary-faced oiler smiled in full sympathy. Previously to the foundering, by the way, the oiler had worked a double watch in the engine-room of the ship.

"Take her easy now, boys," said the captain. "Don't spend yourselves. If we have to run a surf you'll need all your strength, because we'll sure have to swim for it. Take your time."

Slowly the land arose from the sea. From a black line it became a line of black and a line of white—trees and sand. Finally the captain said that he could make out a house on the shore. "That's the house of refuge, sure," said the cook. "They'll see us before long, and come out after us."

The distant lighthouse reared high. "The keeper ought to be able to make us out now, if he's looking through a glass," said the captain. "He'll notify the life-saving people."

"None of those other boats could have got ashore to give word of this wreck," said the oiler, in a low voice, "else the life-boat would be out hunting us."

Slowly and beautifully the land loomed out of the sea. The wind came again. It had veered from the north-east to the south-east. Finally a new sound struck the ears of the men in the boat. It was the low thunder of the surf on the shore. "We'll never be able to make the lighthouse now," said the captain. "Swing her head a little more north, Billie."

"A little more north, sir," said the oiler.

Whereupon the little boat turned her nose once more down the wind, and all but the oarsman watched the shore grow. Under the influence of this expansion doubt and direful apprehension were leaving the minds of the men. The management of the boat was still most absorbing, but it could not prevent a quiet cheerfulness. In an hour, perhaps, they would be ashore.

Their backbones had become thoroughly used to balancing in the boat, and they now rode this wild colt of a dinghy like circus men. The correspondent thought that he had been drenched to the skin, but happening to feel in the top pocket of his coat, he found therein eight cigars. Four of them were soaked with sea-water; four were perfectly scatheless. After a search, somebody produced three dry matches; and thereupon the four waifs rode impudently in their little boat and, with an assurance of an impending rescue shining in their eyes, puffed at the big cigars, and judged well and ill of all men. Everybody took a drink of water.

IV

"Cook," remarked the captain, "there don't seem to be any signs of life about your house of refuge."

"No," replied the cook. "Funny they don't see us!"

A broad stretch of lowly coast lay before the eyes of the men. It was of low dunes topped with dark vegetation. The roar of the surf was plain, and sometimes they could see the white lip of a wave as it spun up the beach. A tiny house was blocked out black upon the sky. Southward, the slim lighthouse lifted its little grey length.

Tide, wind, and waves were swinging the dinghy northward. "Funny they don't see us," said the men.

The surf's roar was here dulled, but its tone was nevertheless thunderous and mighty. As the boat swam over the great rollers the men sat listening to this roar. "We'll swamp sure," said everybody.

It is fair to say here that there was not a life-saving station within twenty miles in either direction; but the men did not know this fact, and in consequence they made dark and opprobrious remarks concerning the eyesight of the nation's life-savers. Four scowling men sat in the dinghy and surpassed records in the invention of epithets.

"Funny they don't see us."

The light-heartedness of a former time had completely faded. To their sharpened minds it was easy to conjure pictures of all kinds of incompetency and blindness and, indeed, cowardice. There was the shore of the populous land, and it was bitter and bitter to them that from it came no sign.

"Well," said the captain, ultimately, "I suppose we'll have to make a try for ourselves. If we stay out here too long, we'll none of us have strength left to swim after the boat swamps."

And so the oiler, who was at the oars, turned the boat straight for the shore. There was a sudden tightening of muscles. There was some thinking.

"If we don't all get ashore," said the captain—"if we don't all get ashore, I suppose you fellows know where to send news of my finish?"

They then briefly exchanged some addresses and admonitions. As for the reflections of the men, there was a great deal of rage in them. Perchance they might be formulated thus: "If I am going to be drowned—if I am going to be drowned—if I am going to be drowned, why, in the name of the seven mad gods who rule the sea, was I allowed to come thus far and contemplate sand and trees? Was I brought here merely to have my nose dragged away as I was about to nibble the sacred cheese of life? It is preposterous. If this old ninny-woman, Fate, cannot do better than this, she should be deprived of the management of men's fortunes. She is an old hen who knows not her intention. If she has decided to drown me, why did she not do it in the beginning and save me all this trouble? The whole affair is absurd.—But no; she cannot mean to drown me. She dare not drown me. She cannot drown me. Not after all this work." Afterward the man might have had an impulse to shake his fist at the clouds. "Just you drown me, now, and then hear what I call you!"

The billows that came at this time were more formidable. They seemed always just about to break and roll over the little boat in a turmoil of foam. There was a preparatory and long growl in the speech of them. No mind unused to the sea would have concluded that the dinghy could ascend these sheer heights in time. The shore was still afar. The oiler was a wily surfman. "Boys," he said swiftly, "she won't live three minutes more, and we're too far out to swim. Shall I take her to sea again, Captain?"

"Yes, go ahead!" said the captain.

This oiler, by a series of quick miracles and fast and steady oarsmanship, turned the boat in the middle of the surf and took her safely to sea again.

There was a considerable silence as the boat bumped over the furrowed sea to deeper water. Then somebody in gloom spoke: "Well, anyhow, they must have seen us from the shore by now."

The gulls went in slanting flight up the wind toward the grey, desolate east. A squall, marked by dingy clouds and clouds brick-red like smoke from a burning building, appeared from the south-east.

"What do you think of those life-saving people? Ain't they peaches?"

"Funny they haven't seen us."

"Maybe they think we're out here for sport! Maybe they think we're fishin'. Maybe they think we're damned fools."

It was a long afternoon. A changed tide tried to force them southward, but wind and wave said northward. Far ahead, where coastline, sea, and sky formed their mighty angle, there were little dots which seemed to indicate a city on the shore.

"St. Augustine?"

The captain shook his head. "Too near Mosquito Inlet."

And the oiler rowed, and then the correspondent rowed; then the oiler rowed. It was a weary business. The human back can become the seat of more aches and pains than are registered in books for the composite anatomy of a regiment. It is a limited area, but it can become the theatre of innumerable muscular conflicts, tangles, wrenches, knots, and other comforts.

"Did you ever like to row, Billie?" asked the correspondent.

"No," said the oiler, "hang it!"

When one exchanged the rowing-seat for a place in the bottom of the boat, he suffered a bodily depression that caused him to be careless of everything save an obligation to wiggle one finger. There was cold sea-water swashing to and fro in the boat, and he lay in it. His head, pillowed on a thwart, was within an inch of the swirl of a wave-crest, and sometimes a particularly obstreperous sea came inboard and drenched him once more. But these matters did not annoy him. It is almost certain that if the boat had capsized he would have tumbled comfortably out upon the ocean as if he felt sure that it was a great soft mattress.

"Look! There's a man on the shore!"

"Where?"

"There! See 'im? See 'im?"

"Yes, sure! He's walking along."

"Now he's stopped. Look! He's facing us!"

"He's waving at us!"

"So he is! By thunder!"

"Ah, now we're all right! Now we're all right! There'll be a boat out here for us in half an hour."

"He's going on. He's running. He's going up to that house there."

The remote beach seemed lower than the sea, and it required a searching glance to discern the little black figure. The captain saw a floating stick, and they rowed to it. A bath towel was by some weird chance in the boat, and, tying this on the stick, the captain waved it. The oarsman did not dare turn his head, so he was obliged to ask questions.

"What's he doing now?"

"He's standing still again. He's looking, I think.—There he goes again—toward the house.—Now he's stopped again."

"Is he waving at us?"

"No, not now; he was, though."

"Look! There comes another man!"

"He's running."

"Look at him go, would you!"

"Why, he's on a bicycle. Now he's met the other man. They're both waving at us. Look!"

"There comes something up the beach."

"What the devil is that thing?"

"Why, it looks like a boat."

"Why, certainly, it's a boat."

"No, it's on wheels."

"Yes, so it is. Well, that must be the life-boat. They drag them along shore on a wagon."

"That's the life-boat, sure."

"No, by God, it's—it's an omnibus."

"I tell you it's a life-boat."

"It is not! It's an omnibus. I can see it plain. See? One of these big hotel omnibuses."

"By thunder, you're right. It's an omnibus, sure as fate. What do you suppose they are doing with an omnibus? Maybe they are going around collecting the life-crew, hey?"

"That's it, likely. Look! There's a fellow waving a little black flag. He's standing on the steps of the omnibus. There come those other two fellows. Now they're all talking together. Look at the fellow with the flag. Maybe he ain't waving it!"

"That ain't a flag, is it? That's his coat. Why, certainly, that's his coat."

"So it is; it's his coat. He's taken it off and is waving it around his head. But would you look at him swing it!"

"Oh, say, there isn't any life-saving station there. That's just a winter-resort hotel omnibus that has brought over some of the boarders to see us drown."

"What's that idiot with the coat mean? What's he signalling, anyhow?"

"It looks as if he were trying to tell us to go north. There must be a life-saving station up there."

"No; he thinks we're fishing. Just giving us a merry hand. See? Ah, there, Willie!"

"Well, I wish I could make something out of those signals. What do you suppose he means?"

"He don't mean anything; he's just playing."

"Well, if he'd just signal us to try the surf again, or to go to sea and wait, or go north, or go south, or go to hell, there would be some reason in it. But look at him! He just stands there and keeps his coat revolving like a wheel. The ass!"

"There come more people."

"Now there's quite a mob. Look! Isn't that a boat?"

"Where? Oh, I see where you mean. No, that's no boat."

"That fellow is still waving his coat."

"He must think we like to see him do that. Why don't he quit it? It don't mean anything.

"I don't know. I think he is trying to make us go north. It must be that there's a life-saving station there somewhere."

"Say, he ain't tired yet. Look at 'im wave!"

"Wonder how long he can keep that up. He's been revolving his coat ever since he caught sight of us. He's an idiot. Why aren't they getting men to bring a boat out? A fishing-boat—one of those big yawls—could come out here all right. Why don't he do something?"

"Oh, it's all right now."

"They'll have a boat out here for us in less than no time, now that they've seen us."

A faint yellow tone came into the sky over the low land. The shadows on the sea slowly deepened. The wind bore coldness with it, and the men began to shiver.

"Holy smoke!" said one, allowing his voice to express his impious mood, "if we keep on monkeying out here! If we've got to flounder out here all night!"

"Oh, we'll never have to stay here all night! Don't you worry. They've seen us now, and it won't be long before they'll come chasing out after us."

The shore grew dusky. The man waving a coat blended gradually into this gloom, and it swallowed in the same manner the omnibus and the group of people. The spray, when it dashed uproariously over the side, made the voyagers shrink and swear like men who were being branded.

"I'd like to catch the chump who waved the coat. I feel like socking him one, just for luck."

"Why? What did he do?"

"Oh, nothing, but then he seemed so damned cheerful."

In the meantime the oiler rowed, and then the correspondent rowed, and then the oiler rowed. Grey-faced and bowed forward, they mechanically, turn by turn, plied the leaden oars. The form of the lighthouse had vanished from the southern horizon, but finally a pale star appeared, just lifting from the sea. The streaked saffron in the west passed before the all-merging darkness, and the sea to the east was black. The land had vanished, and was expressed only by the low and drear thunder of the surf.

"If I am going to be drowned—if I am going to be drowned—if I am going to be drowned, why, in the name of the seven mad gods who rule the sea, was I allowed to come thus far and contemplate sand and trees? Was I brought here merely to have my nose dragged away as I was about to nibble the sacred cheese of life?"

The patient captain, drooped over the water-jar, was sometimes obliged to speak to the oarsman.

"Keep her head up! Keep her head up!"

"Keep her head up, sir." The voices were weary and low.

This was surely a quiet evening. All save the oarsman lay heavily and listlessly in the boat's bottom. As for him, his eyes were just capable of noting the tall black waves that swept forward in a most sinister silence, save for an occasional subdued growl of a crest.

The cook's head was on a thwart, and he looked without interest at the water under his nose. He was deep in other scenes. Finally he spoke. "Billie," he murmured, dreamfully, "what kind of pie do you like best?"

V

"Pie?" said the oiler and the correspondent, agitatedly. "Don't talk about those things, blast you!"

"Well," said the cook, "I was just thinking about ham sandwiches and—"

A night on the sea in an open boat is a long night. As darkness settled finally, the shine of the light, lifting from the sea in the south, changed to full gold. On the northern horizon a new light appeared, a small bluish gleam on the edge of the waters. These two lights were the furniture of the world. Otherwise there was nothing but waves.

Two men huddled in the stern, and distances were so magnificent in the dinghy that the rower was enabled to keep his feet partly warm by thrusting them under his companions. Their legs indeed extended far under the rowing-seat until they touched the feet of the captain forward. Sometimes, despite the efforts of the tired oarsman, a wave came piling into the boat, an icy wave of the night, and the chilling water soaked them anew. They would twist their bodies for a moment and groan, and sleep the dead sleep once more, while the water in the boat gurgled about them as the craft rocked.

The plan of the oiler and the correspondent was for one to row until he lost the ability, and then arouse the other from his seawater couch in the bottom of the boat.

The oiler plied the oars until his head drooped forward and the overpowering sleep blinded him; and he rowed yet afterward. Then he touched a man in the bottom of the boat, and called his name. "Will you spell me for a little while?" he said, meekly.

"Sure, Billie," said the correspondent, awaking and dragging himself to a sitting position. They exchanged places carefully, and the oiler, cuddling down in the seawater at the cook's side, seemed to go to sleep instantly.

The particular violence of the sea had ceased. The waves came without snarling. The obligation of the man at the oars was to keep the boat headed so that the tilt of the rollers would not capsize her, and to preserve her from filling when the crests rushed past. The black waves were silent and hard to be seen in the darkness. Often one was almost upon the boat before the oarsman was aware.

In a low voice the correspondent addressed the captain. He was not sure that the captain was awake, although this iron man seemed to be always awake. "Captain, shall I keep her making for that light north, sir?"

The same steady voice answered him. "Yes. Keep it about two points off the port bow."

The cook had tied a life-belt around himself in order to get even the warmth which this clumsy cork contrivance could donate, and he seemed almost stove-like when a rower, whose teeth invariably chattered wildly as soon as he ceased his labour, dropped down to sleep.

The correspondent, as he rowed, looked down at the two men sleeping underfoot. The cook's arm was around the oiler's shoulders, and, with their fragmentary clothing and haggard faces, they were the babes of the sea—a grotesque rendering of the old babes in the wood.

Later he must have grown stupid at his work, for suddenly there was a growling of water, and a crest came with a roar and a swash into the boat, and it was a wonder that it did not set the cook afloat in his life-belt. The cook continued to sleep, but the oiler sat up, blinking his eyes and shaking with the new cold.

"Oh, I'm awful sorry, Billie," said the correspondent, contritely.

"That's all right, old boy," said the oiler, and lay down again and was asleep.

Presently it seemed that even the captain dozed, and the correspondent thought that he was the one man afloat on all the oceans. The wind had a voice as it came over the waves, and it was sadder than the end.

There was a long, loud swishing astern of the boat, and a gleaming trail of phosphorescence, like blue flame, was furrowed on the black waters. It might have been made by a monstrous knife.

Then there came a stillness, while the correspondent breathed with open mouth and looked at the sea.

Suddenly there was another swish and another long flash of bluish light, and this time it was alongside the boat, and might almost have been reached with an oar. The correspondent saw an enormous fin speed like a shadow through the water, hurling the crystalline spray and leaving the long glowing trail.

The correspondent looked over his shoulder at the captain. His face was hidden, and he seemed to be asleep. He looked at the babes of the sea. They certainly were asleep. So, being bereft of sympathy, he leaned a little way to one side and swore softly into the sea.

But the thing did not then leave the vicinity of the boat. Ahead or astern, on one side or the other, at intervals long or short, fled the long sparkling streak, and there was to be heard the *whirroo* of the dark fin. The speed and power of the thing was greatly to be admired. It cut the water like a gigantic and keen projectile.

The presence of this biding thing did not affect the man with the same horror that it would if he had been a picnicker. He simply looked at the sea dully and swore in an undertone.

Nevertheless, it is true that he did not wish to be alone with the thing. He wished one of his companions to awake by chance and keep him company with it. But the captain hung motionless over the water-jar, and the oiler and the cook in the bottom of the boat were plunged in slumber.

VI

"If I am going to be drowned—if I am going to be drowned—if I am going to be drowned, why, in the name of the seven mad gods who rule the sea, was I allowed to come thus far and contemplate sand and trees?"

During this dismal night, it may be remarked that a man would conclude that it was really the intention of the seven mad gods to drown him, despite the abominable injustice of it. For it was certainly an abominable injustice to drown a man who had worked so hard, so hard. The man felt it would be a crime most unnatural. Other people had drowned at sea since galleys swarmed with painted sails, but still—

When it occurs to a man that nature does not regard him as important, and that she feels she would not maim the universe by disposing of him, he at first wishes to throw bricks at the temple, and he hates deeply the fact that there are no bricks and no temples. Any visible expression of nature would surely be pelleted with his jeers.

Then, if there be no tangible thing to hoot, he feels, perhaps, the desire to confront a personification and indulge in pleas, bowed to one knee, and with hands supplicant, saying, "Yes, but I love myself."

A high cold star on a winter's night is the word he feels that she says to him. Thereafter he knows the pathos of his situation.

The men in the dinghy had not discussed these matters, but each had, no doubt, reflected upon them in silence and according to his mind. There was seldom any expression upon their faces save the general one of complete weariness. Speech was devoted to the business of the boat.

To chime the notes of his emotion, a verse mysteriously entered the correspondent's head. He had even forgotten this verse, but it suddenly was in his mind.

A soldier of the Legion lay dying in Algiers;
There was lack of woman's nursing, there was dearth of woman's tears:
But a comrade stood beside him, and he took that comrade's hand,
And he said, "I never more shall see my own, my native land."

In his childhood the correspondent had been made acquainted with the fact that a soldier of the Legion lay dying in Algiers, but he had never regarded the fact as important. Myriads of his schoolfellows had informed him of the soldier's plight, but the dinning had naturally ended by making him perfectly indifferent. He had never considered it his affair that a soldier of the Legion lay dying in Algiers, nor had it appeared to him as a matter for sorrow. It was less to him than the breaking of a pencil's point.

Now, however, it quaintly came to him as a human, living thing. It was no longer merely a picture of a few throes in the beast of a poet, meanwhile drinking tea and warming his feet at the grate; it was an actuality—stern, mournful, and fine.

The correspondent plainly saw the soldier. He lay on the sand with his feet out straight and still. While his pale left hand was upon his chest in an attempt to thwart the going of his life, the blood came between his fingers. In the far Algerian distance, a city of low square forms was set against a sky that was faint with the last sunset hues. The correspondent, plying the oars and dreaming of the slow and slower movements of the lips of the soldier, was moved by a profound and perfectly impersonal comprehension. He was sorry for the soldier of the Legion who lay dying in Algiers.

The thing which had followed the boat and waited had evidently grown bored at the delay. There was no longer to be heard the slash of the cutwater, and there was no longer the flame of the long trail. The light in the north still glimmered, but it was apparently no nearer to the boat. Sometimes the boom of the surf rang in the correspondent's ears, and he turned the craft seaward then and rowed harder. Southward, someone had evidently built a watch fire on the beach. It was too low and too far to be seen, but it made a shimmering, roseate reflection upon the bluff in back of it, and this could be discerned from the boat. The wind came stronger, and sometimes a wave suddenly raged out like a mountain cat, and there was to be seen the sheen and sparkle of a broken crest.

The captain, in the bow, moved on his water-jar and sat erect. "Pretty long night," he observed to the correspondent. He looked at the shore. "Those life-saving people take their time."

"Did you see that shark playing around?"

"Yes. I saw him. He was a big fellow, all right."

"Wish I had known you were awake."

Later the correspondent spoke into the bottom of the boat. "Billie!" There was a slow and gradual distanglement. "Billie, will you spell me?"

"Sure," said the oiler.

As soon as the correspondent touched the cold, comfortable sea-water in the bottom of the boat and had huddled close to the cook's life-belt he was deep in sleep, despite the fact that his teeth played all the popular airs. This sleep was so good to him that it was but a moment before he heard a voice call his name in a tone that demonstrated the last stages of exhaustion. "Will you spell me?

"Sure, Billie."

The light in the north had mysteriously vanished, but the correspondent took his course from the wide-awake captain.

Later in the night they took the boat farther out to sea, and the captain directed the cook to take one oar at the stern and keep the boat facing the seas. He was to call out if he should hear the thunder of the surf. This plan enabled the oiler and the correspondent to get respite together. "We'll give those boys a chance to get into shape again," said the captain. They curled down and, after a few preliminary chatterings and trembles, slept once more the dead sleep. Neither knew they had bequeathed to the cook the company of another shark, or perhaps the same shark.

As the boat caroused on the waves, spray occasionally bumped over the side and gave them a fresh soaking, but this had no power to break their repose. The ominous slash of the wind and the water affected them as it would have affected mummies.

"Boys," said the cook, with the notes of every reluctance in his voice, "she's drifted in pretty close. I guess one of you had better take her to sea again." The correspondent, aroused, heard the crash of the toppled crests.

As he was rowing, the captain gave him some whiskey-and-water, and this steadied the chills out of him. "If I ever get ashore and anybody shows me even a photograph of an oar—"

At last there was a short conversation.

"Billie!—Billie, will you spell me?"

"Sure," said the oiler.

VII

When the correspondent again opened his eyes, the sea and the sky were each of the grey hue of the dawning. Later, carmine and gold was painted upon the waters. The morning appeared finally, in its splendour, with a sky of pure blue, and the sunlight flamed on the tips of the waves.

On the distant dunes were set many little black cottages, and a tall white windmill reared above them. No man, nor dog, nor bicycle appeared on the beach. The cottages might have formed a deserted village.

The voyagers scanned the shore. A conference was held in the boat. "Well," said the captain, "if no help is coming, we might better try a run through the surf right away. If we stay out here much longer we will be too weak to do anything for ourselves at all." The others silently acquiesced in this reasoning. The boat was headed for the beach. The correspondent wondered if none ever ascended the tall wind-tower, and if then they never looked seaward. This tower was giant, standing with its back to the plight of the ants. It represented in a degree, to the correspondent, the serenity of nature amid the struggles of the individual—nature in the wind, and nature in the vision of men. She did not seem cruel to him then, nor beneficent, nor treacherous, nor wise. But she was indifferent, flatly indifferent. It is, perhaps, plausible that a man in this situation, impressed with the unconcern of the universe, should see the innumerable flaws of his life, and have them taste wickedly in his mind, and wish for another chance. A distinction between right and wrong seems absurdly clear to him, then, in his new ignorance of the grave-edge, and he understands that if he were given another opportunity he would mend his conduct and his words, and be better and brighter during an introduction or at tea.

"Now, boys," said the captain,"she is going to swamp sure. All we can do is to work her in as far as possible, and then when she swamps, pile out and scramble for the beach. Keep cool now, and don't jump until she swamps sure."

The oiler took the oars. Over his shoulders he scanned the surf. "Captain," he said, "I think I'd better bring her about and keep her head-on to the seas and back her in."

"All right, Billie," said the captain. "Back her in." The oiler swung the boat then, and, seated in the stern, the cook and the correspondent were obliged to look over their shoulders to contemplate the lonely and indifferent shore.

The monstrous inshore rollers heaved the boat high until the men were again enabled to see the white sheets of water scudding up the slanted beach. "We won't get in very close," said the captain. Each time a man could wrest his attention from the rollers, he turned his glance toward the shore, and in the expression of the eyes during this contemplation there was a singular quality. The correspondent, observing the others, knew that they were not afraid, but the full meaning of their glances was shrouded.

As for himself, he was too tired to grapple fundamentally with the fact. He tried to coerce his mind into thinking of it, but the mind was dominated at this time by the muscles, and the muscles said they did not care. It merely occurred to him that if he should drown it would be a shame.

There were be no hurried words, no pallor, no plain agitation. The men simply looked at the shore. "Now, remember to get well clear of the boat when you jump," said the captain.

Seaward the crest of a roller suddenly fell with a thunderous crash, and the long white comber came roaring down upon the boat.

"Steady now," said the captain. The men were silent. They turned their eyes from the shore to the comber and waited. The boat slid up the incline, leaped at the furious top, bounced over it, and swung down the long back of the wave. Some water had been shipped, and the cook bailed it out.

But the next crest crashed also. The tumbling, boiling flood of white water caught the boat and whirled it almost perpendicular. Water swarmed in from all sides. The correspondent had his hands on the gunwale at this time, and when the water entered at that place he swiftly withdrew his fingers, as if he objected to wetting them.

The little boat, drunken with this weight of water, reeled and snuggled deeper into the sea.

"Bail her out, cook! Bail her out!" said the captain.

"All right, Captain," said the cook.

"Now, boys, the next one will do us for sure," said the oiler. "Mind to jump clear of the boat."

The third wave moved forward, huge, furious, implacable. It fairly swallowed the dinghy, and almost simultaneously the men tumbled into the sea. A piece of life-belt had lain in the bottom of the boat, and as the correspondent went overboard he held this to his chest with his left hand.

The January water was icy, and he reflected immediately that it was colder than he had expected to find it off the coast of Florida. This appeared to his dazed mind as a fact important enough to be noted at the time. The coldness of the water was sad; it was tragic. This fact was somehow mixed and confused with his opinion of his own situation, so that it seemed almost a proper reason for tears. The water was cold.

When he came to the surface he was conscious of little but the noisy water. Afterward he saw his companions in the sea. The oiler was ahead in the race. He was swimming strongly and rapidly. Off to the correspondent's left, the cook's great white and corked back bulged out of the water; and in the rear the captain was hanging with his one good hand to the keel of the overturned dinghy.

There is a certain immovable quality to a shore, and the correspondent wondered at it amid the confusion of the sea.

It seemed also very attractive; but the correspondent knew that it was a long journey, and he paddled leisurely. The piece of life-preserver lay under him, and sometimes he whirled down the incline of a wave as if he were on a hand-sled.

But finally he arrived at a place in the sea where travel was beset with difficulty. He did not pause swimming to inquire what manner of current had caught him, but there his progress ceased. The shore was set before him like a bit of scenery on a stage, and he looked at it and understood with his eyes each detail of it.

As the cook passed, much farther to the left, the captain was calling to him, "Turn over on your back, cook! Turn over on your back and use the oar."

"All right, sir." The cook turned on his back, and, paddling with an oar, went ahead as if he were a canoe.

Presently the boat also passed to the left of the correspondent, with the captain clinging with one hand to the keel. He would have appeared like a man raising himself to look over a board fence if it were not for the extraordinary gymnastics of the boat. The correspondent marvelled that the captain could still hold to it.

They passed on nearer to shore—the oiler, the cook, the captain—and following them went the water-jar, bouncing gaily over the seas.

The correspondent remained in the grip of this strange new enemy—a current. The shore, with its white slope of sand and its green bluff topped with little silent cottages, was spread like a picture before him. It was very near to him then, but he was impressed as one who, in a gallery, looks at a scene from Brittany or Holland.

He thought: "I am going to drown? Can it be possible? Can it be possible? Can it be possible?" Perhaps an individual must consider his own death to be the final phenomenon of nature.

But later a wave perhaps whirled him out of this small deadly current, for he found suddenly that he could again make progress toward the shore. Later still he was aware that the captain, clinging with one hand to the keel of the dinghy, had his face turned away from the shore and toward him, and was calling his name. "Come to the boat! Come to the boat!"

In his struggle to reach the captain and the boat, he reflected that when one gets properly wearied drowning must really be a comfortable arrangement—a cessation of hostilities accompanied by a large degree of relief; and he was glad of it, for the main thing in his mind for some moments had been horror of the temporary agony. He did not wish to be hurt.

Presently he saw a man running along the shore. He was undressing with most remarkable speed. Coat, trousers, shirt, everything flew magically off him.

"Come to the boat!" called the captain.

"All right, Captain." As the correspondent paddled, he saw the captain let himself down to bottom and leave the boat. Then the correspondent performed his one little marvel of the voyage. A large wave caught him and flung him with ease and supreme speed completely over the boat and far beyond it. It struck him even then as an event in gymnastics and a true miracle of the sea. An overturned boat in the surf is not a plaything to a swimming man.

The correspondent arrived in water that reached only to his waist, but his condition did not enable him to stand for more than a moment. Each wave knocked him into a heap, and the undertow pulled at him.

Then he saw the man who had been running and undressing, and undressing and running, come bounding into the water. He dragged ashore the cook, and then waded toward the captain; but the captain waved him away and sent him to the correspondent. He was naked—naked as a tree in winter; but a halo was about his head, and he shone like a saint. He gave a strong pull, and a long drag, and a bully heave at the correspondent's hand. The correspondent, schooled in the minor formulae, said, "Thanks, old man." But suddenly the man cried, "What's that?" He pointed a swift finger. The correspondent said, "Go."

In the shallows, face downward, lay the oiler. His forehead touched sand that was periodically, between each wave, clear of the sea.

The correspondent did not know all that transpired afterward. When he achieved safe ground he fell, stiking the sand with each particular part of his body. It was as if he had dropped from a roof, but the thud was grateful to him.

It seemed that instantly the beach was populated with men with blankets, clothes, and flasks, and women with coffee pots and all the remedies sacred to their minds. The welcome of the land to the men from the sea was warm and generous; but a still and dripping shape was carried slowly up the beach, and the land's welcome for it could only be the different and sinister hospitality of the grave.

When it came night, the white waves paced to and fro in the moonlight, and the wind brought the sound of the great sea's voice to the men on the shore, and they felt that they could then be interpreters.

There are many ways to think about this story, not only in its relationship to the experience that stimulated it, but also to the intricacies of it as an artistic work of fiction. By now you have had enough experience with the topic of truth and its relation to fiction to assess your own response to Crane's two accounts of the wreck of the *Commodore* and the hours at sea in the open boat. You may find some suggestions useful, however, for your extended considerations of the story.

One way for the whole class to work toward an understanding of the story is to have each working group take one of the seven sections of "The Open Boat." Each of you should first complete Log Entry 9 and then meet in your groups.

*Lo*g Entry 9

Individually, make some notes, using the following as a guide.

1. Examine the literal aspect of your section. What happens? How is this action related to the action of the whole? (Note what went on before and after your section.) Write out a literal account of your section in a few sentences.

2. Look at the newspaper account ("Stephen Crane's Own Story") and see whether you can find anything there that provides specific information for your section. Did Crane use a phrase from the newspaper account that appears in the story? Jot down anything you find.

3. Imagine that you are a fifth passenger on the boat. What do you feel during this part of the experience? Toward the ocean? Toward the other people in the boat? Toward yourself? Do you identify with the correspondent? With another of the characters? Write this response in a few sentences. At what point (lines and phrases) are these feelings most intense? Jot them down.

Collaborating

As a group, create a graphic. Reach some consensus as to the content and effect of your section of the story. To create your group graphic, follow these steps:

1. Sketch a graphic that captures the experience of your section. If there are shifts in time, setting, or mood, show them. You are not illustrating the action; you are representing it—literally, metaphorically, symbolically. Use color meaningfully; that is, decide which colors are most appropriate for which events or feelings.

2. Select words, phrases, whole lines from the story and weave them into your graphic to validate your interpretation.

3. Put the finishing touches on your graphic. Remember that your goals are

   - to convey the total impact and effect of your section.

   - to convey any changes in the section or shifts in your own understanding, or to show the static quality of your section.

   - to show how your section relates to the whole—how it furthers what preceded and leads to what follows.

4. Together, compose a statement (no more than a page) about your graphic, telling how it reflects the meaning and effect of your section. Write this on a single page, with your section number at the top.

If your classroom has a large bulletin board, you should clear it before you begin to share your graphics with the whole class. The Section I group should put its graphic up on the board, using it as a touchstone to talk about the interpretation of that section and ways that the newspaper account relates to it. Section I group members should field questions from the class. The written statement prepared by the group should then be placed on the board beside the graphic. Each section should follow in turn until the entire story is presented visually, with opportunities for questions and elaborations in group discussion.

Work in Progress

Choose one or more of the following options to draft for your writing folder.

- Write an interpretive paper in which you examine the meaning and effect of your section in relation to the whole.

- Select a situation you were involved in, and write up an account of this situation for a newspaper. You might select a time when you were part of a closely knit group of people who cooperated to achieve an end, which may or may not have worked out as you planned. Or, you might select a time when you battled against the elements of nature.

- Remaining true to the factual aspects of the incident as described in your account, write a short story based on the event.

Building Your Course Portfolio

Your portfolio will contain your final reflective essay from this chapter (guidelines are in the second Portfolio Entry below) and a selection of other writing from this chapter as well. It may also include graphics or works in other modes, such as video or film, if you used these media. It should represent your best work and provide the basis for an assessment of your work over the course of this chapter. You may want to review the introduction to the portfolio in the first chapter of this book.

Portfolio Entry

Alone or with a partner, create a graphic portraying, with color, design, and words, how truth fits into your thinking about nonfiction and fiction, about art and life. Use quotations from and references to the stories, poems, and essays in this section as well as those you have read earlier. You may want to include references to other art forms—painting, music, dance, or film.

Portfolio Entry

Explore the connections you see between art and life. Use your graphic and your own experiences to probe into this question. This should be an explorative, reflective essay, not an argumentative one. Ground your ideas in examples, but let your own ideas determine the organization and style of your paper. For this essay, because it should represent your best thinking and writing, use your writing group to test early drafts and give you feedback on whether you are communicating your ideas effectively.

Revising and Editing

Using your log, works in progress from your writing folder, and portfolio entries, look at all the possibilities you have generated during your work in this chapter. Some pieces may well be finished already; other promising pieces may just be notations in your log. Because the portfolio represents your best work, the texts you want to share with others, your goal now is to select those pieces that you want to work on. You may want to include some of your log entries as well as the poems, memory writings, stories, or essays that you wrote. Include responses to different works of literature so that your portfolio will be representative of your writing in the whole chapter.

5

Transforming Texts Through Performance

*T*heater-goers today generally expect plays to entertain them or to arouse their emotions in some way. Most modern plays do this by presenting real people in real situations. Although plays have not always been realistic, they have, throughout the history of drama, been concerned with representing our deepest emotions— both tragic and comic. Appearing first as the dramatization of ancient rituals closely associated with the worship of a god or gods, plays evolved through the comedies and tragedies of William Shakespeare, to the seemingly nonsensical Theater of the Absurd, to the realism of today. Today, we can expect to see plays from every age and of every kind; a seventeenth-century farce might be playing next door to a contemporary American musical. And next week, there might be a classical Greek drama opening on one of those stages.

Through their dramas, playwrights have taken stories old and new and transformed them into performances wherein the stories live anew each time they are performed. Playwrights have adapted and modified characters and events to fit their own time, audience, and/or purpose. When the plays are produced, directors often transform the texts further by changing settings or cutting lines. These transformations are part of the process of creation.

In this chapter, you will have opportunities to explore the idea of transformation through performance by reading a classic tragedy and some modern poetic transformations of the story. *Oedipus Rex* by Sophocles, a famous Greek play, tells a story of love and fear, of blindness and truth. Throughout the ages, playwrights and poets have transformed this story into texts that address the issues of their time against the background of universal concepts such as fate vs. free will and knowledge vs. blindness.

In reading this play, you will have opportunities to think about how we, as readers, create texts out of the texts of others. That is, as we read, we build the story in our minds, and the stories that each of us creates are slightly different because they depend in part on the background experiences we bring to the text. As a reader or a viewer of *Oedipus Rex,* we follow the events, knowing what the outcome will be. In addition to being an observer of the events, we may also take an active role in questioning the values, assumptions, judgments, or beliefs that we see acted out. But what we see and what we question are partially determined by who we are; that is one important element of interpretation.

We may also search out the stories that are not told in the text. For example, there are certainly stories within the story of Oedipus that are not dealt with in the play—Jocasta's story, their children's stories, and the stories of those people who must have been touched daily by the lives of the royal family. You will be encouraged to imagine those additional stories and to respond to the stories that modern poets have created to fill the gaps that the text leaves for us.

Reading as a Performer

In addition to your response to the words of the play, another important element of interpretation is the means by which you experience the play. In this chapter, you will be reading the play from an angle that may not be familiar to you—as a performer. As you see it here, the play is merely words on the page. Yet you know that plays are more than that. When reading plays, you must stage them in "the theater of your mind," using your imagination to see the action and to hear the dialogue. When plays are performed, directors and actors interpret the playwright's words, scenic designers set them on a meaningful stage, and audiences provide necessary feedback for live performers. The play on the page is like the tip of an iceberg; you see only one-tenth of what is there while the other nine-tenths remains submerged. As a performer, you will focus on the entire iceberg. We will call the remaining nine-tenths of the play the "subtext." Subtext includes all of the nuances of meaning—pacing, tone, emphasis, silence, and blocking—that make a performance more than just written dialogues.

Before you read the play, spend a little time with the following exercises that will introduce you to some tools for reading as a performer.

Reading the Subtext

In this section, improvisations will give you a chance to study the subtext of a playwright's words. As you know, the way that words are spoken is often more important than the words themselves. Try saying "I didn't mean it" in the following ways:

- as a small child who realizes he has hurt his sister's feelings

- as a sulky teenager forced to apologize to an adult

- as a surprised adult who discovers her 6-year-old son has taken something she said literally

- as a lover apologizing for saying or doing something hurtful

Even in saying those four words, you may have found yourself changing several aspects of the subtext—pacing, tone, emphasis, and silence. When you add actors on a stage, you also consider the grouping of those people—where they stand in relation to others. Actors and directors call that "blocking." After brief explanations of each of these elements, you will get a chance to try them out in a scene.

The *pacing* or timing of a line or scene influences the mood or atmosphere. You could, of course, read lines as rapidly as possible to get through the play. Or, you could read them all the same way. But you wouldn't be reading as a performer if you did that. Performers and directors know that pacing is a powerful tool for revealing what is going on inside the actors in a situation at any given time. To better understand this, you might compare pacing to the tempo of a song. Even without the words, you know whether a song is upbeat or in a minor key. You know the mood the songwriter wants to express from the rhythm of the song before you even hear the lyrics. As you read lines of a play, be conscious of the effect you can create through varied pacing.

The sound of your voice expresses your attitude toward your subject—either a person or situation. This attitude is often called *tone.* Usually equated with emotions, tone may be described as happy, sad, jubilant, satiric, ironic, resigned, and so forth. For example, lines may be said in a laughing, menacing, matter-of-fact, or surprised way.

Collaborating

Work in small groups of three or four.

1. Quickly brainstorm with two or three other students as many words as you can that describe emotions. All of you should write

down all of the words on a sheet of paper. See how many you
can get in five minutes.

2. Check with other groups, either informally or in class discussion,
to get words you didn't think of.

*P*erformance

Choose a partner and write a ten-line dialogue (five lines per person) that demonstrates two tones. For example, you might have an
employer firing an employee who was consistently late to work. The
employer will probably speak angrily while the employee may offer
numerous excuses in a whining tone or agree with the employer in
a resigned tone. Present your dialogues to the class and have others
guess what tone you are using. (Be conscious, also, of the variations in pacing used by each pair. It is difficult to separate one aspect of the subtext from another, except for ease of description.)

Just as you will not read every line at the same rate or in the
same tone, you should not read every word with the same degree of
emphasis. Scenes should appear to be building to a climax, and
your use of emphasis can create that tension. You can achieve emphasis with your voice through stressing particular words, varying
your pace, and pausing at significant points.

*P*erformance

Read aloud the following speech by Cyrano de Bergerac. You may be
familiar with the story of Cyrano from reading the play or from seeing Steve Martin's adaptation of the story in the film *Roxanne*. If
you have read the play, you know that Cyrano is a seventeenth-
century swordsman, poet, and philosopher who would seem to
have everything. However, he feels no woman will ever love him

because of his huge nose. If you have seen only the film *Roxanne,*
you still know how Cyrano feels about his "distinctive feature."

As you read aloud, concentrate on building the emotional intensity
with which the speech ends. You'll need to vary your tone, pace, and
emphasis on individual words or phrases throughout the speech.

Cyrano de Bergerac

Edmond Rostand, translated by Brian Hooker

My old friend, look at me,
And tell me how much hope remains for me
With this protuberance! Oh I have no more
Illusions! Now and then bah! I may grow
Tender, walking alone in the blue cool
Of evening, through some garden fresh with flowers
After the benediction of the rain;
My poor big devil of a nose inhales
April . . . and so I follow with my eyes
Where some boy, with a girl upon his arm,
Passes a patch of silver . . . and I feel
Somehow, I wish I had a woman too,
Walking with little steps under the moon,
And holding my arm so, and smiling. Then
I dream—and I forget. . . . And then I see
The shadow of my profile on the wall!

In achieving emphasis, you probably used *silence.* Effectively em-
ployed, silence can give the audience time to react to a situation,
emphasize the line that has just gone before, or provide suspense
that prepares us for the next line. In comedy, silence also gives the
audience a chance to laugh. Used properly, it signals or gives the
audience permission to laugh at the previous line or situation. A
poorly done comedy leaves silences that are either too long or too
short. How do you know how long to be silent? In comedy, it's a
matter of practice and a feeling for the timing. In drama, there is at
least one guideline—the more powerful the preceding line or action,
the longer the silence should be.

From your play-viewing experiences, you may already realize
that the manner in which an actor moves, the gestures used, and

even the part of the stage on which he or she stands all indicate subtle qualities of the character and contribute to the meaning of the play. Although these movements and groupings should look natural, they have all been carefully planned as the directors and actors rehearse the *blocking*.

Before deciding on the blocking, a director sketches a rough design of the acting area, indicating entrances, exits, and placement of furniture or other objects. Given the shape of the stage where the play will be performed, directors plan each actor's steps with a purpose, visualizing the play as a series of stage pictures. Usually the director tries to make sure that the actor who is speaking gets the visual attention. To create a center of attention, directors can use some of the following techniques:

- Specify the actor's body position. Facing the audience calls more attention to the actor. Standing is usually more powerful than sitting, and sitting is more powerful than lying down.

- Direct the other actors to look at the center of interest. The audience's eyes will focus there, too.

- Put the speaking actor in a strong area of the stage. The drawing on the next page shows the nine areas of a proscenium arch stage and their relative strength. In drama terminology, "down" is closest to the audience, and "right" and "left" are from the actors' point of view. Some people feel that areas of the stage have emotional value and that certain scenes should be played in those areas. You need not follow slavishly these guidelines for areas of the stage—directors don't—but they are offered as a starting point. You could adapt them, too, if you're using a different setup where the audience is seated on three or four sides of the stage.

Down Center: climactic scenes where emotions explode

Up Center: scenes of dignity, royalty, or formality

Down Right: love scenes

Down Left: routine scenes, soliloquies, scenes to build tension

Up Right: eavesdropping or foreshadowing events

Up Left: horror scenes, ghosts, unreality

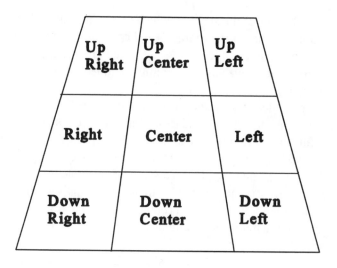

Just as the actor's stage position communicates certain meanings, so does the actor's relationship to other actors. For example, two people sitting on a couch will sit differently depending on whether they are gossips, lovers, or enemies. You will have an opportunity to experiment with some of these blocking ideas as you read *Oedipus Rex* and the poems that follow.

*R*eading *Oedipus Rex*

Oedipus Rex explores ideas about a person's place in the universe and relationships between people. Sophocles, in the fashion of Greeks of his time, gives his words much weight. The play is mostly talk—even the goriest scenes take place offstage and are described by a messenger. To a modern reader, this may not seem very exciting, but we can experience the same recognition of human emotions— expectation, love, frustration, fear, and despair—as the fifth-century Greek audience did. Although they probably knew the basic story of the play before they came to the theater, they were interested in how the playwright would work out the hows and whys of the transformation of the traditional story. Sophocles wanted his viewers actually to *experience* the working out of fate as they understood that individuals cannot always know everything that they seek to know.

Reading a classic play presents some challenges and opportunities that reading a modern play does not. First, we must try to put ourselves in the seats of audience members who lived nearly 2,500 years ago—a daunting task in itself. We cannot really know what they knew or think as they thought. In fact, our view of the Greek people has been shaped by historians and others who have read the writings they left behind and studied the culture, but we can never re-create their experience.

So, why do the plays of Aeschylus, Sophocles, Euripides, and Aristophanes continue to be read and performed? Because they offer us insights into our own character, just as they did the Greeks 2,500 years ago. Although cultural trappings, literary styles, and theaters may change, drama then, just as drama now, dealt with basic human emotions—jealousy, fear, pride, determination, love, revenge. Besides, we all want to see the working out of a good story. *Oedipus Rex* has it all.

In addition to its universal themes, you will probably notice some aspects of the play that are uniquely Greek. If you view these as opportunities for a modern director, rather than as obstacles for a modern reader, you may begin to understand why this play was popular in the theatrical contests of the time.

You may know that Greek drama, from which we get many of our own theatrical traditions, actually evolved from choral festivals, where groups of men sang or chanted odes (a form of lyric poem) to the god Dionysus. Eventually, the narrative element in such odes took precedence, becoming what we would recognize as a *play*. By Sophocles' time, three actors performed all of the speaking parts, assisted by the chorus, a remnant from the drama's origins, and possibly attended by a number of "extras." The chorus, led by a single person (the *choragos* in this translation), provided a commentary on the play's characters and actions, raising questions about what was to come and sending entreaties up to the gods. In *Oedipus Rex,* the chorus represents ordinary citizens, who comment on events as they unfold. All of the actors were mature men who wore masks and long robes. Their appearance, their relationship to the other characters, and their dialogue indicated whether they were playing the role of a man or a woman.

The traditional staging for a Greek play makes it ideal for classroom reading and performance because it doesn't require much movement. Consider a modern outdoor amphitheater or arena and the sound and lighting equipment it takes to stage a concert or play in such a setting—the modern technology required to amplify voices and movements, to make them bigger than life. Now think of the same amphitheater 2,500 years ago, without such equipment. How might actors and chorus in Athens stage a drama, keeping the audience rooted for hours to unyielding stone benches?

Not all technology needs to be electronic to be effective. The Greeks created solutions from materials at hand. Plays were performed during the day so no special lighting effects were necessary. Actors wore shoes with built-up soles (*buskins*) that made them tall enough so that even those sitting farthest away could see them—and some of the audience members could be quite distant in amphitheaters that held up to 15,000!

To create the illusion of several different characters, the three professional actors had to change appearance and mannerisms for each character. To make the task easier, they wore masks. So that everyone could hear, masks were built with small megaphones to amplify the actor's voice. As you might expect, this heavy equipment made movement somewhat difficult.

Because the Greeks felt that drama should provide a heightened view of life, the slow movement added to the regal nature of the entire play. Actors spoke in poetry and their gestures were large and deliberate.

The Story of the Play

The Greek audience probably would have known the story of Oedipus, which goes as follows. Because of a curse on his grandfather, Labdakos, all of his descendants are fated to die tragic deaths. Oedipus, doomed to kill his father and marry his mother, is taken away as an infant and left to die on a hillside. A kind-hearted shepherd takes him in and raises him as his own son. When the adolescent Oedipus hears of the prophecy, he runs away from the people he believes to be his mother and father. On the road he meets an elderly man with few attendants and, in a quarrel over the right-of-way, Oedipus kills the man and all except one attendant. Oedipus does not know that the dead man is King Laios, his real father. Oedipus goes on to Thebes, where the Sphinx has besieged the town, allowing no one to enter who cannot answer her riddle: What creature walks on four legs in the morning, two in the afternoon, and three at night, and moves most slowly when it has the most feet? Only Oedipus escapes death by knowing that the answer is "Man," who begins life by crawling, continues unsupported, and relies on a cane in old age. Saving the city, Oedipus receives the throne from a grateful Thebes and, with it, as was the custom of the times, the recently widowed queen Iokaste. (In some translations, her name is spelled Jocasta.)

Many years later, the kingdom of Thebes is plague-ridden, and the Oracle at Delphi has said that the cause is the unsolved murder of King Laios. To lift the curse from the city, the murder must be avenged. Where do the necessary clues lie? Here in Thebes, the oracle indicates; their discovery requires no more than an attentive search.

The First Reading

Reading the play aloud will require more than an average-length class period. Depending on your experience with reading plays, you might want to read through the first time primarily to get a sense of the story. If so, omit the choral odes, even though they are rich with emotion and reaction. They should not be omitted in the next reading of the play, but you can get an initial sense of the story without them on your first reading. Then, as you reread, try to determine what the choral odes add to the theme of the play.

When you read aloud *Oedipus Rex,* you might arrange your chairs to create a stage in the classroom. What will the acting area look like? Where will the entrances and exits be? There are brief directions at the beginning of the play, but you'll need to add details in your mind or your classroom as you read.

We have provided a few prompts—questions that may guide your initial reading. If you find it helpful to stop at points in your reading and spend a few minutes reflecting on the play in writing, look for the prompts at the end of the play (Log Entry 1) before you begin reading. If you prefer to read without interruption the first time, you may want to omit the prompts for now.

Oedipus Rex
Sophocles

Characters

OEDIPUS, King of Thebes, supposed son of Polybos and Merope, King and
    Queen of Corinth
IOKASTE, wife of Oedipus and widow of the late King Laios
KREON, brother of Iokaste, a prince of Thebes
TEIRESIAS, a blind seer who serves Apollo

PRIEST
MESSENGER, from Corinth
SHEPHERD, former servant of Laios
SECOND MESSENGER, from the palace
CHORUS OF THEBAN ELDERS
CHORAGOS, leader of the Chorus
ANTIGONE and ISMENE, young daughters of Oedipus and Iokaste. They
    appear in the Exodus but do not speak.
SUPPLIANTS, GUARDS, SERVANTS

THE SCENE. Before the palace of OEDIPUS, *King of Thebes. A central door
and two lateral doors open onto a platform which runs the length of the facade. On the platform, right and left, are altars; and three steps lead down
into the orchestra, or chorus-ground. At the beginning of the action these
steps are crowded by suppliants who have brought branches and chaplets of
olive leaves and who sit in various attitudes of despair.* OEDIPUS *enters.*

Prologue

OEDIPUS. My children, generations of the living
    In the line of Kadmos,[1] nursed at his ancient hearth:
    Why have you strewn yourselves before these altars
    In supplication, with your boughs and garlands?
    The breath of incense rises from the city   5
    With a sound of prayer and lamentation.
                                Children,
    I would not have you speak through messengers,
    And therefore I have come myself to hear you—
    I, Oedipus, who bear the famous name.
    (*To a* PRIEST) You, there, since you are eldest in the company,   10
    Speak for them all, tell me what preys upon you,
    Whether you come in dread, or crave some blessing:
    Tell me, and never doubt that I will help you
    In every way I can; I should be heartless
    Were I not moved to find you suppliant here.   15

PRIEST. Great Oedipus, O powerful king of Thebes!
    You see how all the ages of our people
    Cling to your altar steps: here are boys
    Who can barely stand alone, and here are priests
    By weight of age, as I am a priest of God,   20
    And young men chosen from those yet unmarried;

[1]Legendary founder of Thebes.

As for the others, all that multitude,
They wait with olive chaplets in the squares,
At the two shrines of Pallas,[2] and where Apollo[3]
Speaks in the glowing embers.   25
                      Your own eyes
Must tell you: Thebes is tossed on a murdering sea
And can not lift her head from the death surge.
A rust consumes the buds and fruits of the earth;
The herds are sick; children die unborn,
And labor is vain. The god of plague and pyre   30
Raids like detestable lightning through the city,
And all the house of Kadmos is laid waste,
All emptied, and all darkened: Death alone
Battens upon the misery of Thebes.

You are not one of the immortal gods, we know;   35
Yet we have come to you to make our prayer
As to the man surest in mortal ways
And wisest in the ways of God. You saved us
From the Sphinx,[4] that flinty singer, and the tribute
We paid to her so long; yet you were never   40
Better informed than we, nor could we teach you:
A god's touch, it seems, enabled you to help us.

Therefore, O mighty power, we turn to you:
Find us our safety, find us a remedy,
Whether by counsel of the gods or of men.   45
A king of wisdom tested in the past
Can act in a time of troubles, and act well.
Noblest of men, restore
Life to your city! Think how all men call you
Liberator for your boldness long ago;   50
Ah, when your years of kingship are remembered,
Let them not say *We rose, but later fell*—
Keep the State from going down in the storm!
Once, years ago, with happy augury,
You brought us fortune; be the same again!   55

---

[2]Athena, goddess of wisdom, patroness of Athens.
[3]God of the sun, music, and medicine.
[4]A winged monster, with the body of a lion and the breasts and head of a woman.

No man questions your power to rule the land:
But rule over men, not over a dead city!
Ships are only hulls, high walls are nothing,
When no life moves in the empty passageways.

OEDIPUS. Poor children! You may be sure I know   60
    All that you longed for in your coming here.
    I know that you are deathly sick; and yet,
    Sick as you are, not one is as sick as I.
    Each of you suffers in himself alone
    His anguish, not another's; but my spirit   65
    Groans for the city, for myself, for you.

    I was not sleeping, you are not waking me.
    No, I have been in tears for a long while
    And in my restless thought walked many ways.
    In all my search I found one remedy,   70
    And I have adopted it: I have sent Kreon,
    Son of Menoikeus, brother of the queen,
    To Delphi, Apollo's place of revelation,
    To learn there, if he can,
    What act or pledge of mine may save the city.   75
    I have counted the days, and now, this very day,
    I am troubled, for he has overstayed his time.
    What is he doing? He has been gone too long.
    Yet whenever he comes back, I should do ill
    Not to take any action the god orders.   80

PRIEST. It is a timely promise. At this instant
    They tell me Kreon is here.

OEDIPUS.   O Lord Apollo!
    May his news be fair as his face is radiant!

PRIEST. Good news, I gather! he is crowned with bay,
    The chaplet is thick with berries.

OEDIPUS.   We shall soon know;   85

He is near enough to hear us now.

    (*Enter* KREON.)
                      O prince:
    Brother: son of Menoikeus:
    What answer do you bring us from the god?

KREON. A strong one. I can tell you, great afflictions
　　　Will turn out well, if they are taken well.   90

OEDIPUS. What was the oracle? These vague words
　　　Leave me still hanging between hope and fear.

KREON. Is it your pleasure to hear me with all these
　　　Gathered around us? I am prepared to speak,
　　　But should we not go in?

OEDIPUS.　　　　　　　　　Speak to them all,   95
　　　It is for them I suffer, more than for myself.

KREON. Then I will tell you what I heard at Delphi.
　　　In plain words
　　　The god commands us to expel from the land of Thebes
　　　An old defilement we are sheltering.   100
　　　It is a deathly thing, beyond cure;
　　　We must not let it feed upon us longer.

OEDIPUS. What defilement? How shall we rid ourselves of it?

KREON. By exile or death, blood for blood. It was
　　　Murder that brought the plague-wind on the city.   105

OEDIPUS. Murder of whom? Surely the god has named him?

KREON. My lord: Laios once ruled this land,
　　　Before you came to govern us.

OEDIPUS.　　　　　　　　　I know;
　　　I learned of him from others; I never saw him.

KREON. He was murdered; and Apollo commands us now   110
　　　To take revenge upon whoever killed him.

OEDIPUS. Upon whom? Where are they? Where shall we find a clue
　　　To solve that crime, after so many years?

KREON. Here in this land, he said. Search reveals
　　　Things that escape an inattentive man.   115

OEDIPUS. Tell me: Was Laios murdered in his house,
　　　Or in the fields, or in some foreign country?

KREON. He said he planned to make a pilgrimage.
　　　He did not come home again.

OEDIPUS.   And there was no one,
    No witness, no companion, to tell what happened?   120

KREON. They were all killed but one, and he got away
    So frightened that he could remember one thing only.

OEDIPUS. What was that one thing? One may be the key
    To everything, if we resolve to use it.

KREON. He said that a band of highwaymen attacked them,   125
    Outnumbered them, and overwhelmed the king.

OEDIPUS. Strange, that a highwayman should be so daring—
    Unless some faction here bribed him to do it.

KREON. We thought of that. But after Laios' death
    New troubles arose and we had no avenger.   130

OEDIPUS. What troubles could prevent your hunting down the killers?

KREON. The riddling Sphinx's song
    Made us deaf to all mysteries but her own.

OEDIPUS. Then once more I must bring what is dark to light.
    It is most fitting that Apollo shows,   135
    As you do, this compunction for the dead.
    You shall see how I stand by you, as I should.
    Avenging this country and the god as well,
    And not as though it were for some distant friend,
    But for my own sake, to be rid of evil.   140
    Whoever killed King Laios might—who knows?—
    Lay violent hands even on me—and soon.
    I act for the murdered king in my own interest.

    Come, then, my children: leave the altar steps,
    Lift up your olive boughs!
                One of you go   145
    And summon the people of Kadmos to gather here.
    I will do all that I can; you may tell them that.

    (*Exit a* PAGE.)

    So, with the help of God,
    We shall be saved—or else indeed we are lost.

PRIEST. Let us rise, children. It was for this we came,   150
    And now the king has promised it.

Phoibus⁵ has sent us an oracle; may he descend
Himself to save us and drive out the plague.

(*Exeunt* OEDIPUS *and* KREON *into the palace by the central door. The*
PRIEST *and the* SUPPLIANTS *disperse right and left. After a short pause the*
CHORUS *enters the orchestra.*)

Parados⁶

Strophe 1

CHORUS. What is God singing in his profound
    Delphi of gold and shadow?   155
    What oracle for Thebes, the sunwhipped city?
    Fear unjoints me, the roots of my heart tremble.
    Now I remember, O Healer, your power, and wonder:
    Will you send doom like a sudden cloud, or weave it
    Like nightfall of the past?   160
    Speak to me, tell me, O
    Child of golden Hope, immortal Voice.

Antistrophe 1

    Let me pray to Athene, the immortal daughter of Zeus,
    And to Artemis her sister
    Who keeps her famous throne in the market ring,   165
    And to Apollo, archer from distant heaven—
    O gods, descend! Like three streams leap against
    The fires of our grief, the fires of darkness;
    Be swift to bring us rest!
    As in the old time from the brilliant house   170
    Of air you stepped to save us, come again!

Strophe 2

    Now our afflictions have no end,
    Now all our stricken host lies down
    And no man fights off death with his mind;
    The noble plowland bears no grain,   175
    And groaning mothers can not bear—
    See, how our lives like birds take wing,
    Like sparks that fly when a fire soars,
    To the shore of the god of evening.

⁵Phoebus Apollo, god of the sun, whose oracle was at Delphi.
⁶The Parados is the poetic song of the entering Chorus.

Antistrophe 2

> The plague burns on, it is pitiless,   180
> Though pallid children laden with death
> Lie unwept in the stony ways,
> And old gray women by every path
> Flock to the strand about the altars
> There to strike their breasts and cry   185
> Worship of Phoibus in wailing prayers:
> Be kind, God's golden child!

Strophe 3

> There are no swords in this attack by fire,
> No shields, but we are ringed with cries.
> Send the besieger plunging from our homes   190
> Into the vast sea-room of the Atlantic
> Or into the waves that foam eastward of Thrace—
> For the day ravages what the night spares—
> Destroy our enemy, lord of the thunder!
> Let him be riven by lightning from heaven!   195

Antistrophe 3

> Phoibus Apollo, stretch the sun's bowstring,
> That golden cord, until it sing for us,
> Flashing arrows in heaven!
>   Artemis, Huntress,
> Race with flaring lights upon our mountains!
> O scarlet god, O golden-banded brow,   200
> O Theban Bacchos in a storm of Maenads,[7]

(Enter OEDIPUS, *center.)*

> Whirl upon Death, that all the Undying hate!
> Come with blinding torches, come in joy!

Scene 1

OEDIPUS. Is this your prayer? It may be answered. Come,
> Listen to me, act as the crisis demands,   205
> And you shall have relief from all these evils.

---

[7]Bacchos: the god of wine and revelry. Maenads were female attendants of the god.

Until now I was a stranger to this tale,
As I had been a stranger to the crime.
Could I track down the murderer without a clue?
But now, friends,   210
As one who became a citizen after the murder,
I make this proclamation to all Thebans:
If any man knows by whose hand Laios, son of Labdakos,
Met his death, I direct that man to tell me everything,
No matter what he fears for having so long withheld it.   215
Let it stand as promised that no further trouble
Will come to him, but he may leave the land in safety.
Moreover: If anyone knows the murderer to be foreign,
Let him not keep silent: he shall have his reward from me.
However, if he does conceal it; if any man   220
Fearing for his friend or for himself disobeys this edict,
Hear what I propose to do:

I solemnly forbid the people of this country,
Where power and throne are mine, ever to receive that man
Or speak to him, no matter who he is, or let him   225
Join in sacrifice, lustration,[8] or in prayer.
I decree that he be driven from every house,
Being, as he is, corruption itself to us: the Delphic
Voice of Apollo has pronounced this revelation.
Thus I associate myself with the oracle   230
And take the side of the murdered king.

As for the criminal, I pray to God—
Whether it be a lurking thief, or one of a number—
I pray that that man's life be consumed in evil and
    wretchedness.
And as for me, this curse applies no less   235
If it should turn out that the culprit is my guest here,
Sharing my hearth.
                                    You have heard the penalty.
I lay it on you now to attend to this
For my sake, for Apollo's, for the sick
Sterile city that heaven has abandoned.   240
Suppose the oracle had given you no command:
Should this defilement go uncleansed for ever?

[8]lustration: ritual purification.

You should have found the murderer: your king,
A noble king, had been destroyed!

           Now I,
Having the power that he held before me,   245
Having his bed, begetting children there
Upon his wife, as he would have, had he lived—
Their son would have been my children's brother,
If Laios had had luck in fatherhood!
(And now his bad fortune has struck him down)—   250
I say I take the son's part, just as though
I were his son, to press the fight for him
And see it won! I'll find the hand that brought
Death to Labdakos' and Polydoros' child,
Heir of Kadmos' and Agenor's line.[9]   255
And as for those who fail me,
May the gods deny them the fruit of the earth,
Fruit of the womb, and may they rot utterly!
Let them be wretched as we are wretched, and worse!

For you, for loyal Thebans, and for all   260
Who find my actions right, I pray the favor
Of justice, and of all the immortal gods.

CHORAGOS.[10] Since I am under oath, my lord, I swear
    I did not do the murder, I can not name
    The murderer. Phoibos ordained the search: 265
    Why did he not say who the culprit was?

OEDIPUS. An honest question. But no man in the world
    Can make the gods do more than the gods will.

CHORAGOS. There is an alternative, I think—

OEDIPUS.   Tell me.
    Any or all, you must not fail to tell me.   270

CHORAGOS. A lord clairvoyant to the lord Apollo,
    As we all know, is the skilled Teiresias.
    One might learn much about this from him, Oedipus.

---

[9]The royal line of descent: Kadmos=Polydoros=Labdakos=Laios=Oedipus.
[10]The Choragos is the leader of the Chorus.

OEDIPUS. I am not wasting time:
    Kreon spoke of this, and I have sent for him—   275
    Twice, in fact; it is strange that he is not here.

CHORAGOS. The other matter—the old report—seems useless.

OEDIPUS. What was that? I am interested in all reports.

CHORAGOS. The king was said to have been killed by highwaymen.

OEDIPUS. I know. But we have no witnesses to that.   280

CHORAGOS. If the killer can feel a particle of dread,
    Your curse will bring him out of hiding!

OEDIPUS.   No.
    The man who dared that act will fear no curse.

    (*Enter the blind seer* TEIRESIAS, *led by a* PAGE.)

CHORAGOS. But there is one man who may detect the criminal.
    This is Teiresias, this is the holy prophet   285
    In whom, alone of all men, truth was born.

OEDIPUS. Teiresias: seer: student of mysteries,
    Of all that's taught and all that no man tells,
    Secrets of Heaven and secrets of the earth:
    Blind though you are, you know the city lies   290
    Sick with plague: and from this plague, my lord,
    We find that you alone can guard or save us.

    Possibly you did not hear the messengers?
    Apollo, when we sent to him,
    Sent us back word that this great pestilence   295
    Would lift, but only if we established clearly
    The identity of those who murdered Laios.
    They must be killed or exiled.
                            Can you use
    Birdflight[11] or any art of divination
    To purify yourself, and Thebes, and me   300
    From this contagion? We are in your hands.
    There is no fairer duty
    Than that of helping others in distress.

[11]The flight patterns of birds were used to foretell the future.

TEIRESIAS. How dreadful knowledge of the truth can be
    When there's no help in truth! I knew this well,   305
    But did not act on it: else I should have not come.

OEDIPUS. What is troubling you? Why are your eyes so cold?

TEIRESIAS. Let me go home. Bear your own fate, and I'll
    Bear mine. It is better so: trust what I say.

OEDIPUS. What you say is ungracious and unhelpful   310
    To your native country. Do not refuse to speak.

TEIRESIAS. When it comes to speech, your own is neither temperate
    Nor opportune. I wish to be more prudent.

OEDIPUS. In God's name, we all beg you—

TEIRESIAS.   You are all ignorant.
    No; I will never tell you what I know.   315
    Now it is my misery; then, it would be yours.

OEDIPUS. What! You do know something, and will not tell us?
    You would betray us all and wreck the State?

TEIRESIAS. I do not intend to torture myself, or you.
    Why persist in asking? You will not persuade me.   320

OEDIPUS. What a wicked old man you are! You'd try a stone's
    Patience! Out with it! Have you no feeling at all?

TEIRESIAS. You call me unfeeling. If you could only see
    The nature of your own feelings . . .

OEDIPUS.   Why,
    Who would not feel as I do? Who could endure   325
    Your arrogance toward the city?

TEIRESIAS.   What does it matter?
    Whether I speak or not, it is bound to come.

OEDIPUS. Then, if "it" is bound to come, you are bound to tell me.

TEIRESIAS. No, I will not go on. Rage as you please.

OEDIPUS. Rage? Why not!
                    And I'll tell you what I think: 330
    You planned it, you had it done, you all but
    Killed him with your own hands: if you had eyes,
    I'd say the crime was yours, and yours alone.

TEIRESIAS. So? I charge you, then,
    Abide by the proclamation you have made: 335
    From this day forth
    Never speak again to these men or to me;
    You yourself are the pollution of this country.

OEDIPUS. You dare say that! Can you possibly think you have
    Some way of going free, after such insolence?   340

TEIRESIAS. I have gone free. It is the truth sustains me.

OEDIPUS. Who taught you shamelessness? It was not your craft.

TEIRESIAS. You did. You made me speak. I did not want to.

OEDIPUS. Speak what? Let me hear it again more clearly.

TEIRESIAS. Was it not clear before? Are you tempting me?   345

OEDIPUS. I did not understand it. Say it again.

TEIRESIAS. I say that you are the murderer whom you seek.

OEDIPUS. Now twice you have spat out infamy. You'll pay for it!

TEIRESIAS. Would you care for more? Do you wish to be really angry?

OEDIPUS. Say what you will. Whatever you say is worthless.   350

TEIRESIAS. I say you live in hideous shame with those
    Most dear to you. You can not see the evil.

OEDIPUS. Can you go on babbling like this for ever?

TEIRESIAS. I can, if there is power in truth.

OEDIPUS.   There is:
    But not for you, not for you,   355
    You sightless, witless, senseless, mad old man!

TEIRESIAS. You are the madman. There is no one here
    Who will not curse you soon, as you curse me.

OEDIPUS. You child of total night! I would not touch you;
    Neither would any man who sees the sun.   360

TEIRESIAS. True: it is not from you my fate will come.
    That lies within Apollo's competence,
    As it is his concern.

OEDIPUS.   Tell me, who made
   These fine discoveries? Kreon? or someone else?

TEIRESIAS. Kreon is no threat. You weave your own doom.   365

OEDIPUS. Wealth, power, craft of statemanship!
   Kingly position, everywhere admired!
   What savage envy is stored up against these,
   If Kreon, whom I trusted, Kreon my friend,
   For this great office which the city once   370
   Put in my hands unsought—if for this power
   Kreon desires in secret to destroy me!

   He has brought this decrepit fortune-teller, this
   Collector of dirty pennies, this prophet fraud—
   Why, he is no more clairvoyant that I am!
                                        Tell us: 375
   Has your mystic mummery ever approached the truth?
   When that hellcat the Sphinx was performing here,
   What help were you to these people?
   Her magic was not for the first man who came along:
   It demanded a real exorcist. Your birds—   380
   What good were they? or the gods, for the matter of that?
   But I came by,
   Oedipus, the simple man, who knows nothing—
   I thought it out for myself, no birds helped me!
   And this is the man you think you can destroy,   385
   That you may be close to Kreon when he's king!
   Well, you and your friend Kreon, it seems to me,
   Will suffer most. If you were not an old man,
   You would have paid already for your plot.

CHORAGOS. We can not see that his words or yours   390
   Have been spoken except in anger, Oedipus,
   And of anger we have no need. How to accomplish
   The god's will best: that is what most concerns us.

TEIRESIAS. You are a king. But where argument's concerned
   I am your man, as much a king as you.   395
   I am not your servant, but Apollo's.
   I have no need of Kreon or Kreon's name.

   Listen to me. You mock my blindness, do you?
   But I say that you, with both your eyes, are blind:

You can not see the wretchedness of your life,   400
Nor in whose house you live, no, nor with whom.
Who are your father and mother? Can you tell me?
You do not even know the blind wrongs
That you have done them, on earth and in the world below.
But that double lash of your parents' curse will whip you   405
Out of this land some day, with only night
Upon your precious eyes.
Your cries then—where will they not be heard?
What fastness of Kithairon[12] will not echo them?
And that bridal-descant of yours—you'll know it then,   410
The song they sang when you came here to Thebes
And found your misguided berthing.
All this, and more, that you can not guess at now,
Will bring you to yourself among your children.

Be angry, then. Curse Kreon. Curse my words.   415
I tell you, no man that walks upon earth
Shall be rooted out more horribly than you.

OEDIPUS. Am I to bear this from him?—Damnation
        Take you! Out of this place! Out of my sight!

TEIRESIAS. I would not have come at all if you had not asked me.   420

OEDIPUS. Could I have told that you'd talk nonsense, that
        You'd come here to make a fool of yourself, and of me?

TEIRESIAS. A fool? Your parents thought me sane enough.

OEDIPUS. My parents again!—Wait: who were my parents?

TEIRESIAS. This day will give you a father, and break your heart.   425

OEDIPUS. Your infantile riddles! Your damned abracadabra!

TEIRESIAS. You were a great man once at solving riddles.

OEDIPUS. Mock me with that if you like; you will find it true.

TEIRESIAS. It was true enough. It brought about your ruin.

OEDIPUS. But if it saved this town?

TEIRESIAS. (to the PAGE.)   Boy, give me your hand.   430

---

[12]A mountain range near Thebes where the infant Oedipus was left to die.

OEDIPUS. Yes, boy; lead him away.

          —While you are here

We can do nothing. Go; leave us in peace.

TEIRESIAS. I will go when I have said what I have to say.

    How can you hurt me? And I tell you again:

    The man you have been looking for all this time,   435

    The damned man, the murderer of Laios,

    That man is in Thebes. To your mind he is foreign-born,

    But it will soon be shown that he is a Theban,

    A revelation that will fail to please.

                A blind man,

    Who has his eyes now; a penniless man, who is rich now;   440

    And he will go tapping the strange earth with his staff.

    To the children with whom he lives now he will be

    Brother and father—the very same; to her

    Who bore him, son and husband—the very same

    Who came to his father's bed, wet with his father's blood.   445

    Enough. Go think that over.

    If later you find error in what I have said,

    You may say that I have no skill in prophecy.

(*Exit* TEIRESIAS, *led by his* PAGE. OEDIPUS *goes into the palace.*)

Ode 1

Strophe 1

CHORUS. The Delphic stone of prophecies

    Remembers ancient regicide   450

    And a still bloody hand.

    That killer's hour of flight has come.

    He must be stronger than riderless

    Coursers of untiring wind,

    For the son of Zeus[13] armed with his father's thunder   455

    Leaps in lightning after him;

    And the Furies hold his track, the sad Furies.[14]

Antistrophe 1

    Holy Parnassos' peak of snow

    Flashes and blinds that secret man,

[13]Apollo.
[14]Avenging goddesses.

That all shall hunt him down: 460
Though he may roam the forest shade
Like a bull gone wild from pasture
To rage through glooms of stone.
Doom comes down on him; flight will not avail him;
For the world's heart calls him desolate,   465
And the immortal voices follow, for ever follow.

Strophe 2

But now a wilder thing is heard
From the old man skilled at hearing Fate in the wing-beat
    of a bird.
Bewildered as a blown bird, my soul hovers and can not find
Foothold in this debate, or any reason or rest of mind.   470
But no man ever brought—none can bring
Proof of strife between Thebes' royal house,
Labdakos' line, and the son of Polybos;[15]
And never until now has any man brought word
Of Laios' dark death staining Oedipus the King.   475

Antistrophe 2

Divine Zeus and Apollo hold
Perfect intelligence alone of all tales ever told;
And well though this diviner works, he works in his own night;
No man can judge that rough unknown or trust in second sight,
For wisdom changes hands among the wise.   480
Shall I believe my great lord criminal
At a raging word that a blind old man let fall?
I saw him, when the carrion woman faced him of old,
Prove his heroic mind. These evil words are lies.

Scene II

KREON. Men of Thebes: 485
I am told that heavy accusations
Have been brought against me by King Oedipus.

I am not the kind of man to bear this tamely.

If in these present difficulties
He holds me accountable for any harm to him   490
Through anything I have said or done—why, then,

---

[15]Oedipus is mistakenly assumed to be Polybos's son.

I do not value life in this dishonor.
It is not as though this rumor touched upon
Some private indiscretion. The matter is grave.
The fact is that I am being called disloyal   495
To the State, to my fellow citizens, to my friends.

CHORAGOS. He may have spoken in anger, not from his mind.

KREON. But did you not hear him say I was the one
    Who seduced the old prophet into lying?

CHORAGOS. The thing was said; I do not know how seriously.   500

KREON. But you were watching him! Were his eyes steady?
    Did he look like a man in his right mind?

CHORAGOS.   I do not know.
    I can not judge the behavior of great men.
    But here is the king himself.

    (*Enter* OEDIPUS.)

OEDIPUS.   So you dared come back.
    Why? How brazen of you to come to my house,   505
    You murderer!
                Do you think I do not know
    That you plotted to kill me, plotted to steal my throne?
    Tell me, in God's name: am I coward, a fool,
    That you should dream you could accomplish this?
    A fool who could not see your slippery game?   510
    A coward, not to fight back when I saw it?
    You are the fool, Kreon, are you not? Hoping
    Without support or friends to get a throne?
    Thrones may be won or bought: you could do neither.

KREON. Now listen to me. You have talked; let me talk, too.   515
    You can not judge unless you know the facts.

OEDIPUS. You speak well: there is one fact; but I find it hard
    To learn from the deadliest enemy I have.

KREON. That above all I must dispute with you.

OEDIPUS. That above all I will not hear you deny.   520

KREON. If you think there is anything good in being stubborn
    Against all reason, then I say you are wrong.

OEDIPUS. If you think a man can sin against his own kind
    And not be punished for it, I say you are mad.

KREON. I agree. But tell me: what have I done to you?   525

OEDIPUS. You advised me to send for that wizard, did you not?

KREON. I did. I should do it again.

OEDIPUS.   Very well. Now tell me:
    How long has it been since Laios—

KREON.   What of Laios?

OEDIPUS. Since he vanished in that onset by the road?

KREON. It was long ago, a long time.

OEDIPUS.   And this prophet,   530
    Was he practicing here then?

KREON.   He was; and with honor, as now.

OEDIPUS. Did he speak of me at that time?

KREON.   He never did,
    At least, not when I was present.

OEDIPUS.   But . . . the enquiry?
    I suppose you held one?

KREON.   We did, but we learned nothing.

OEDIPUS. Why did the prophet not speak against me then?   535

KREON. I do not know; and I am the kind of man
    Who holds his tongue when he has no facts to go on.

OEDIPUS. There's one fact that you know, and you could tell it.

KREON. What fact is that? If I know it, you shall have it.

OEDIPUS. If he were not involved with you, he could not say   540
    That it was I who murdered Laios.

KREON. If he says that, you are the one that knows it!—
    But now it is my turn to question you.

OEDIPUS. Put your questions. I am no murderer.

KREON. First, then: You married my sister?

OEDIPUS.   I married your sister.   545

KREON. And you rule the kingdom equally with her?

OEDIPUS. Everything that she wants she has from me.

KREON. And I am the third, equal to both of you?

OEDIPUS. That is why I call you a bad friend.

KREON. No. Reason it out, as I have done.   550
    Think of this first: Would any sane man prefer
    Power, with all a king's anxieties,
    To that same power and the grace of sleep?
    Certainly not I.
    I have never longed for the king's power—only his rights.   555
    Would any wise man differ from me in this?
    As matters stand, I have my way in everything
    With your consent, and no responsibilities.
    If I were king, I should be a slave to policy.
    How could I desire a scepter more   560
    Than what is now mine—untroubled influence?
    No, I have not gone mad; I need no honors,
    Except those with the perquisites I have now.
    I am welcome everywhere; every man salutes me,
    And those who want your favor seek my ear,   565
    Since I know how to manage what they ask.
    Should I exchange this ease for that anxiety?
    Besides, no sober mind is treasonable.
    I hate anarchy
    And never would deal with any man who likes it.   570

    Test what I have said. Go to the priestess
    At Delphi, ask if I quoted her correctly.
    And as for this other thing: if I am found
    Guilty of treason with Teiresias,
    Then sentence me to death. You have my word   575
    It is a sentence I should cast my vote for—
    But not without evidence!
                You do wrong
    When you take good men for bad, bad men for good.
    A true friend thrown aside—why, life itself
    Is not more precious!

In time you will know this well: 580
For time, and time alone, will show the just man,
Though scoundrels are discovered in a day.

CHORAGOS. This is well said, and a prudent man would ponder it.
Judgments too quickly formed are dangerous.

OEDIPUS. But is he not quick in his duplicity? 585
And shall I not be quick to parry him?
Would you have me stand still, hold my peace, and let
This man win everything, through my inaction?

KREON. And you want—what is it, then? To banish me?

OEDIPUS. No, not exile. It is your death I want, 590
So that all the world may see what treason means.

KREON. You will persist, then? You will not believe me?

OEDIPUS. How can I believe you?

KREON.   Then you are a fool.

OEDIPUS. To save myself?

KREON.   In justice, think of me.

OEDIPUS. You are evil incarnate.

KREON.   But suppose you are wrong? 595

OEDIPUS. Still I must rule.

KREON.   But not if you rule badly.

OEDIPUS. O city, city!

KREON.   It is my city, too!

CHORAGOS. Now, my lords, be still. I see the queen,
Iokaste, coming from her palace chambers;
And it is time she came, for the sake of you both. 600
This dreadful quarrel can be resolved through her.

(*Enter* IOKASTE.)

IOKASTE. Poor foolish men, what wicked din is this?
With Thebes sick to death, is it not shameful
That you should rake some private quarrel up?

(*To* OEDIPUS.) Come into the house.
                            —And you, Kreon, go now: 605
Let us have no more of this tumult over nothing.

KREON. Nothing? No, sister: what your husband plans for me
    Is one of two great evils: exile or death.

OEDIPUS. He is right.
                    Why, woman I have caught him squarely
    Plotting against my life.

KREON.   No! Let me die   610
    Accurst if ever I have wished you harm!

IOKASTE. Ah, believe it, Oedipus!
    In the name of the gods, respect this oath of his
    For my sake, for the sake of these people here!

Strophe 1

CHORAGOS. Open your mind to her, my lord. Be ruled by her, I
        beg you!   615

OEDIPUS. What would you have me do?

CHORAGOS. Respect Kreon's word. He has never spoken like a fool,
    And now he has sworn an oath.

OEDIPUS.   You know what you ask?

CHORAGOS.   I do.

OEDIPUS.   Speak on, then.

CHORAGOS. A friend so sworn should not be baited so,
    In blind malice, and without final proof.   620

OEDIPUS. You are aware, I hope, that what you say
    Means death for me, or exile at the least.

Strophe 2

CHORAGOS. No, I swear by Helios, first in heaven!
        May I die friendless and accurst,
            The worst of deaths, if ever I meant that!   625
                It is the withering fields
                    That hurt my sick heart:
                Must we bear all these ills,
                    And now your bad blood as well?

OEDIPUS. Then let him go. And let me die, if I must,   630
    Or be driven by him in shame from the land of Thebes.
    It is your unhappiness, and not his talk,
    That touches me.
             As for him—
    Wherever he goes, hatred will follow him.

KREON. Ugly in yielding, as you were ugly in rage!   635
    Natures like yours chiefly torment themselves.

OEDIPUS. Can you not go? Can you not leave me?

KREON.   I can.
    You do not know me; but the city knows me,
    And in its eyes I am just, if not in yours.

    (*Exit* KREON.)

Antistrophe 1

CHORAGOS. Lady Iokaste, did you not ask the King to go to his
    chambers?   640

IOKASTE. First tell me what has happened.

CHORAGOS. There was suspicion without evidence; yet it rankled
    As even false charges will.

IOKASTE. On both sides?

CHORAGOS.   On both.

IOKASTE.   But what was said?

CHORAGOS. Oh let it rest, let it be done with!
    Have we not suffered enough?   645

OEDIPUS. You see to what your decency has brought you:
    You have made difficulties where my heart saw none.

Antistrophe 2

CHORAGOS. Oedipus, it is not once only I have told you—
      You must know I should count myself unwise
      To the point of madness, should I now forsake you—   650
        You, under whose hand,
          In the storm of another time,
        Our dear land sailed out free.
        But now stand fast at the helm!

IOKASTE. In God's name, Oedipus, inform your wife as well: 655
    Why are you so set in this hard anger?

OEDIPUS. I will tell you, for none of these men deserves
    My confidence as you do. It is Kreon's work,
    His treachery, his plotting against me.

IOKASTE. Go on, if you can make this clear to me.   660

OEDIPUS. He charges me with the murder of Laios.

IOKASTE. Has he some knowledge? Or does he speak from hearsay?

OEDIPUS. He would not commit himself to such a charge,
    But he has brought in that damnable soothsayer
    To tell his story.

IOKASTE.   Set your mind at rest.   665
    If it is a question of soothsayers, I tell you
    That you will find no man whose craft gives knowledge
    Of the unknowable.
           Here is my proof:
    An oracle was reported to Laios once
    (I will not say from Phoibos himself, but from   670
    His appointed ministers, at any rate)
    That his doom would be death at the hands of his own son—
    His son, born of his flesh and of mine!

    Now, you remember the story: Laios was killed
    By marauding strangers where three highways meet;   675
    But his child had not been three days in this world
    Before the king had pierced the baby's ankles
    And left him to die on a lonely mountainside.

    Thus, Apollo never caused that child
    To kill his father, and it was not for Laios' fate   680
    To die at the hands of his son, as he had feared.
    This is what prophets and prophecies are worth!
    Have no dread of them.
           It is God himself
    Who can show us what he wills, in his own way.

OEDIPUS. How strange a shadowy memory crossed my mind.   685
    Just now while you were speaking; it chilled my heart.

IOKASTE. What do you mean? What memory do you speak of?

OEDIPUS. If I understand you, Laios was killed
   At a place where three roads meet.

IOKASTE.   So it was said;
   We have no later story.

OEDIPUS.   Where did it happen?   690

IOKASTE. Phokis, it is called: at a place where the Theban Way
   Divides into the roads toward Delphi and Daulia.

OEDIPUS. When?

IOKASTE.   We had the news not long before you came
   And proved the right to your succession here.

OEDIPUS. Ah, what net has God been weaving for me?   695

IOKASTE. Oedipus! Why does this trouble you?

OEDIPUS.   Do not ask me yet.
   First, tell me how Laios looked, and tell me
   How old he was.

IOKASTE.   He was tall, his hair just touched
   With white; his form was not unlike your own.

OEDIPUS. I think that I myself may be accurst   700
   By my own ignorant edict.

IOKASTE.   You speak strangely.
   It makes me tremble to look at you, my king.

OEDIPUS. I am not sure that the blind man can not see.
   But I should know better if you were to tell me—

IOKASTE. Anything—though I dread to hear you ask it.   705

OEDIPUS. Was the king lightly escorted, or did he ride
   With a large company, as a ruler should?

IOKASTE. There were five men with him in all: one was a herald;
   And a single chariot, which he was driving.

OEDIPUS. Alas, that makes it plain enough!
                              But who—   710
   Who told you how it happened?

IOKASTE.   A household servant,
   The only one to escape.

OEDIPUS.   And is he still
   A servant of ours?

IOKASTE.   No; for when he came back at last
   And found you enthroned in the place of the dead king,
   He came to me, touched my hand with his, and begged   715
   That I would send him away to the frontier district
   Where only the shepherds go—
   As far away from the city as I could send him.
   I granted his prayer; for although the man was a slave,
   He had earned more than his favor at my hands.   720

OEDIPUS. Can he be called back quickly?

IOKASTE.   Easily.
   But why?

OEDIPUS. I have taken too much upon myself
   Without enquiry; therefore I wish to consult him.

IOKASTE. Then he shall come.
                          But am I not one also
   To whom you might confide these fears of yours?   725

OEDIPUS. That is your right; it will not be denied you,
   Now least of all; for I have reached a pitch
   Of wild foreboding. Is there anyone
   To whom I should sooner speak?

   Polybos of Corinth is my father.   730
   My mother is a Dorian: Merope.
   I grew up chief among the men of Corinth
   Until a strange thing happened—
   Not worth my passion, it may be, but strange.
   At a feast, a drunken man maundering in his cups   735
   Cries out that I am not my father's son!

   I contained myself that night, though I felt anger
   And a sinking heart. The next day I visited
   My father and mother, and questioned them. They stormed,
   Calling it all the slanderous rant of a fool;   740
   And this relieved me. Yet the suspicion

Remained always aching in my mind;
I knew there was talk; I could not rest;
And finally, saying nothing to my parents,
I went to the shrine at Delphi.   745

The god dismissed my question without reply;
He spoke of other things.
                             Some were clear,
Full of wretchedness, dreadful, unbearable:
As, that I should lie with my own mother, breed
Children from whom all men would turn their eyes;   750
And that I should be my father's murderer.

I heard all this, and fled. And from that day
Corinth to me was only in the stars
Descending in that quarter of the sky,
As I wandered farther and farther on my way   755
To a land where I should never see the evil
Sung by the oracle. And I came to this country
Where, so you say, King Laios was killed.

I will tell you all that happened there, my lady.
There were three highways   760
Coming together at a place I passed;
And there a herald came towards me, and a chariot
Drawn by horses, with a man such as you describe
Seated in it. The groom leading the horses
Forced me off the road at his lord's command;   765
But as this charioteer lurched over towards me
I struck him in my rage. The old man saw me
And brought his double goad down upon my head
As I came abreast.
                      He was paid back, and more!
Swinging my club in this right hand I knocked him   770
Out of his car, and he rolled on the ground.
                                I killed him.

I killed them all.
Now if that stranger and Laios were—kin,
Where is a man more miserable than I?
More hated by the gods? Citizen and alien alike   775
Must never shelter me or speak to me—
I must be shunned by all.
                      And I myself

Pronounced this malediction upon myself!

Think of it: I have touched you with these hands,
These hands that killed your husband. What defilement!   780

Am I all evil, then? It must be so,
Since I must flee from Thebes, yet never again
See my own countrymen, my own country,
For fear of joining my mother in marriage
And killing Polybos, my father.
                                    Ah,   785
If I was created so, born to this fate,
Who would deny the savagery of God?

O holy majesty of heavenly powers!
May I never see that day! Never!
Rather let me vanish from the race of men   790
Than know the abomination destined me!

CHORAGOS. We too, my lord, have felt dismay at this.
          But there is hope: you have yet to hear the shepherd.

OEDIPUS. Indeed, I fear no other hope is left me.

IOKASTE. What do you hope from him when he comes?

OEDIPUS.   This much: 795
          If his account of the murder tallies with yours,
          Then I am cleared.

IOKASTE.   What was it that I said
          Of such importance?

OEDIPUS.   Why, "marauders," you said,
          Killed the king, according to this man's story.
          If he maintains that still, if there were several,   800
          Clearly the guilt is not mine: I was alone.
          But if he says one man, singlehanded, did it,
          Then the evidence all points to me.

IOKASTE. You may be sure that he said there were several;
          And can he call back that story now? He can not.   805
          The whole city heard it as plainly as I.
          But suppose he alters some detail of it:
          He can not ever show that Laios' death
          Fulfilled the oracle: for Apollo said

My child was doomed to kill him; and my child—   810
Poor baby!—it was my child that died first.

No. From now on, where oracles are concerned,
I would not waste a second thought on any.

OEDIPUS. You may be right.
                              But come: let someone go
For the shepherd at once. This matter must be settled.   815

IOKASTE. I will send for him.
          I would not wish to cross you in anything,
          And surely not in this.—Let us go in.

(*Exeunt into the palace.*)

Ode II

Strophe 1

CHORUS. Let me be reverent in the ways of right,
          Lowly the paths I journey on;   820
          Let all my words and actions keep
          The laws of the pure universe
          From highest Heaven handed down.
          For Heaven is their bright nurse,
          Those generations of the realms of light;   825
          Ah, never of mortal kind were they begot,
          Nor are they slaves of memory, lost in sheep:
          Their Father is greater than Time, and ages not.

Antistrophe 1

          The tyrant is a child of Pride
          Who drinks from his great sickening cup   830
          Recklessness and vanity,
          Until from his high crest headlong
          He plummets to the dust of hope.
          That strong man is not strong.
          But let no fair ambition be denied;   835
          May God protect the wrestler for the State
          In government, in comely policy,
          Who will fear God, and on His ordinance wait.

Strophe 2

> Haughtiness and the high hand of disdain
> Tempt and outrage God's holy law;   840
> And any mortal who dares hold
> No immortal Power in awe
> Will be caught up in a net of pain:
> The price for which his levity is sold.
> Let each man take due earnings, then,   845
> And keep his hands from holy things,
> And from blasphemy stand apart—
> Else the crackling blast of heaven
> Blows on his head, and on his desperate heart.
> Though fools will honor impious men,   850
> In their cities no tragic poet sings.

Antistrophe 2

> Shall we lose faith in Delphi's obscurities,
> We who have heard the world's core
> Discredited, and the sacred wood
> Of Zeus at Elis praised no more?   855
> The deeds and the strange prophecies
> Must make a pattern yet to be understood.
> Zeus, if indeed you are lord of all,
> Throned in light over night and day,
> Mirror this in your endless mind: 860
> Our masters call the oracle
> Words on the wind, and the Delphic vision blind!
> Their hearts no longer know Apollo,
> And reverence for the gods has died away.

Scene III

(Enter IOKASTE.)

IOKASTE. Princes of Thebes, it has occurred to me   865
> To visit the altars of the gods, bearing
> These branches as a suppliant, and this incense.
> Our king is not himself: his noble soul
> Is overwrought with fantasies of dread,
> Else he would consider   870
> The new prophecies in the light of the old.

He will listen to any voice that speaks disaster,
And my advice goes for nothing.

(*She approaches the altar, right.*)

                             To you, then, Apollo,
Lycean lord, since you are nearest, I turn in prayer.
Receive these offerings, and grant us deliverance   875
From defilement. Our hearts are heavy with fear
When we see our leader distracted, as helpless sailors
Are terrified by the confusion of their helmsman.

(*Enter* MESSENGER.)

MESSENGER. Friends, no doubt you can direct me:
    Where shall I find the house of Oedipus,   880
    Or, better still, where is the king himself?

CHORAGOS. It is this very place, stranger; he is inside.
    This is his wife and mother of his children.

MESSENGER. I wish her happiness in a happy house,
    Blest in all the fulfillment of her marriage.   885

IOKASTE. I wish as much for you: your courtesy
    Deserves a like good fortune. But now, tell me:
    Why have you come? What have you to say to us?

MESSENGER. Good news, my lady, for your house and your husband.

IOKASTE. What news? Who sent you here?

MESSENGER.   I am from Corinth.   890
    The news I bring ought to mean joy for you,
    Though it may be you will find some grief in it.

IOKASTE. What is it? How can it touch us in both ways?

MESSENGER. The word is that the people of the Isthmus
    Intend to call Oedipus to be their king.   895

IOKASTE. But old King Polybos—is he not reigning still?

MESSENGER. No. Death holds him in his sepulchre.

IOKASTE. What are you saying? Polybos is dead?

MESSENGER. If I am not telling the truth, may I die myself.

IOKASTE. (*to a* MAIDSERVANT). Go in, go quickly; tell this
    to your master.   900
    O riddlers of God's will, where are you now!
    This was the man whom Oedipus, long ago,
    Feared so, fled so, in dread of destroying him—
    But it was another fate by which he died.

    (*Enter* OEDIPUS, *center.*)

OEDIPUS. Dearest Iokaste, why have you sent for me?   905

IOKASTE. Listen to what this man says, and then tell me
    What has become of the solemn prophecies.

OEDIPUS. Who is this man? What is his news for me?

IOKASTE. He has come from Corinth to announce your
    father's death!

OEDIPUS. Is it true, stranger? Tell me in your own words.   910

MESSENGER. I can not say it more clearly: the king is dead.

OEDIPUS. Was it by treason? Or by an attack of illness?

MESSENGER. A little thing brings old men to their rest.

OEDIPUS. It was sickness, then?

MESSENGER.   Yes, and his many years.   915

OEDIPUS. Ah!
    Why should a man respect the Pythian hearth, or
    Give heed to the birds that jangle above his head?
    They prophesied that I should kill Polybos,
    Kill my own father; but he is dead and buried,
    And I am here—I never touched him, never,   920
    Unless he died of grief for my departure,
    And thus, in a sense, through me. No. Polybos
    Has packed the oracles off with him underground.
    They are empty words.

IOKASTE.   Had I not told you so?

OEDIPUS. You had; it was my faint heart that betrayed me.   925

IOKASTE. From now on never think of those things again.

OEDIPUS. And yet—must I not fear my mother's bed?

IOKASTE. Why should anyone in this world be afraid,
Since Fate rules us and nothing can be foreseen?
A man should live only for the present day.   930

Have no more fear of sleeping with your mother:
How many men, in dreams, have lain with their mothers!
No reasonable man is troubled by such things.

OEDIPUS. That is true; only—
If only my mother were not still alive!   935
But she is alive. I can not help my dread.

IOKASTE. Yet this news of your father's death is wonderful.

OEDIPUS. Wonderful. But I fear the living woman.

MESSENGER. Tell me, who is this woman that you fear?

OEDIPUS. It is Merope, man; the wife of King Polybos.   940

MESSENGER. Merope? Why should you be afraid of her?

OEDIPUS. An oracle of the gods, a dreadful saying.

MESSENGER. Can you tell me about it or are you sworn to silence?

OEDIPUS. I can tell you, and I will.
Apollo said through his prophet that I was the man   945
Who should marry his own mother, shed his father's blood
With his own hands. And so, for all these years
I have kept clear of Corinth, and no harm has come—
Though it would have been sweet to see my parents again.

MESSENGER. And this is the fear that drove you out of Corinth? 950

OEDIPUS. Would you have me kill my father?

MESSENGER.   As for that
You must be reassured by the news I gave you.

OEDIPUS. If you could reassure me, I would reward you.

MESSENGER. I had that in mind, I will confess: I thought
I could count on you when you returned to Corinth.   955

OEDIPUS. No: I will never go near my parents again.

MESSENGER. Ah, son, you still do not know what you are doing—

OEDIPUS. What do you mean? In the name of God tell me!

MESSENGER. —If these are your reasons for not going home.

OEDIPUS. I tell you, I fear the oracle may come true.   960

MESSENGER. And guilt may come upon you through your parents?

OEDIPUS. That is the dread that is always in my heart.

MESSENGER. Can you not see that all your fears are groundless?

OEDIPUS. Groundless? Am I not my parents' son?

MESSENGER. Polybos was not your father.

OEDIPUS.   Not my father?   965

MESSENGER. No more your father than the man speaking to you.

OEDIPUS. But you are nothing to me!

MESSENGER.   Neither was he.

OEDIPUS. Then why did he call me son?

MESSENGER.   I will tell you:
    Long ago he had you from my hands, as a gift.

OEDIPUS. Then how could he love me so, if I was not his?   970

MESSENGER. He had no children, and his heart turned to you.

OEDIPUS. What of you? Did you buy me? Did you find me by chance?

MESSENGER. I came upon you in the woody vales of Kithairon.

OEDIPUS. And what were you doing there?

MESSENGER.   Tending my flocks.

OEDIPUS. A wandering shepherd?

MESSENGER.   But your savior, son, that day.   975

OEDIPUS. From what did you save me?

MESSENGER.   Your ankles should tell you that.

OEDIPUS. Ah, stranger, why do you speak of that childhood pain?

MESSENGER. I pulled the skewer that pinned your feet together.

OEDIPUS. I have had the mark as long as I can remember.

MESSENGER. That was why you were given the name you bear.   980

OEDIPUS. God! Was it my father or my mother who did it? Tell me!

MESSENGER. I do not know. The man who gave you to me
    Can tell you better than I.

OEDIPUS. It was not you that found me, but another?

MESSENGER. It was another shepherd gave you to me.   985

OEDIPUS. Who was he? Can you tell me who he was?

MESSENGER. I think he was said to be one of Laios' people.

OEDIPUS. You mean the Laios who was king here years ago?

MESSENGER. Yes; King Laios; and the man was one of his herdsmen.

OEDIPUS. Is he still alive? Can I see him?

MESSENGER.   These men here   990
    Know best about such things.

OEDIPUS.   Does anyone here
    Know this shepherd that he is talking about?
    Have you seen him in the fields, or in the town?
    If you have, tell me. It is time things were made plain.

CHORAGOS. I think the man he means is that same shepherd   995
    You have already asked to see. Iokaste perhaps
    Could tell you something.

OEDIPUS.   Do you know anything
    About him, Lady? Is he the man we have summoned?
    Is that the man this shepherd means?

IOKASTE.   Why think of him?
    Forget this herdsman. Forget it all.   1000
    This talk is a waste of time.

OEDIPUS.   How can you say that,
    When the clues to my true birth are in my hands?

IOKASTE. For God's love, let us have no more questioning!
    Is your life nothing to you?
    My own is pain enough for me to bear.   1005

OEDIPUS. You need not worry. Suppose my mother a slave,
    And born of slaves: no baseness can touch you.

IOKASTE. Listen to me, I beg you: do not do this thing!

OEDIPUS. I will not listen; the truth must be made known.

IOKASTE. Everything that I say is for your own good!

OEDIPUS.   My own good   1010
    Snaps my patience, then; I want none of it.

IOKASTE. You are fatally wrong! May you never learn who you are!

OEDIPUS. Go, one of you, and bring the shepherd here.
    Let us leave this woman to brag of her royal name.

IOKASTE. Ah, miserable!   1015
    That is the only word I have for you now.
    That is the only word I can ever have. (*Exit into the palace.*)

CHORAGOS. Why has she left us, Oedipus? Why has she gone
    In such a passion of sorrow? I fear this silence:
    Something dreadful may come of it.

OEDIPUS.   Let it come!   1020
    However base my birth, I must know about it.
    The Queen, like a woman, is perhaps ashamed
    To think of my low origin. But I
    Am a child of Luck; I can not be dishonored.
    Luck is my mother; the passing months, my brothers,   1025
    Have seen me rich and poor.
                      If this is so,
    How could I wish that I were someone else?
    How could I not be glad to know my birth?

Ode III

Strophe

CHORAGOS. If ever the coming time were known
    To my heart's pondering,
                                1030
    Kithairon, now by Heaven I see the torches

At the festival of the next full moon,
And see the dance, and hear the choir sing
A grace to your gentle shade:
Mountain where Oedipus was found,   1035
O mountain guard of a noble race!
May the god who heals us lend his aid,
And let that glory come to pass
For our king's cradling-ground.

Antistrophe

Of the nymphs that flower beyond the years,   1040
Who bore you, royal child,
To Pan of the hills or the timberline Apollo,
Cold in delight where the upland clears,
Or Hermes for whom Kyllene's heights are piled?
Or flushed as evening cloud,   1045
Great Dionysos, roamer of mountains,
He—was it he who found you there,
And caught you up in his own proud
Arms from the sweet god-ravisher
Who laughed by the Muses' fountains?   1050

Scene IV

OEDIPUS. Sirs: though I do not know the man,
    I think I see him coming, this shepherd we want:
    He is old, like our friend here, and the men
    Bringing him seem to be servants of my house.
    But you can tell, if you have ever seen him.   1055

    (*Enter* SHEPHERD *escorted by* SERVANTS.)

CHORAGOS. I know him, he was Laios' man. You can trust him.

OEDIPUS. Tell me first, you from Corinth: is this the shepherd
    We were discussing?

MESSENGER.   This is the very man.

OEDIPUS. (*to* SHEPHERD). Come here. No, look at me. You must
    answer
    Everything I ask.—You belonged to Laios?   1060

SHEPHERD. Yes: born his slave, brought up in his house.

OEDIPUS. Tell me: what kind of work did you do for him?

SHEPHERD. I was a shepherd of his, most of my life.

OEDIPUS. Where mainly did you go for pasturage?

SHEPHERD. Sometimes Kithairon, sometimes the hills near-by.   1065

OEDIPUS. Do you remember ever seeing this man out there?

SHEPHERD. What would he be doing there? This man?

OEDIPUS. This man standing here. Have you ever seen him before?

SHEPHERD. No. At least, not to my recollection.

MESSENGER. And that is not strange, my lord. But I'll refresh   1070
    His memory: he must remember when we two
    Spent three whole seasons together, March to September,
    On Kithairon or thereabouts. He had two flocks;
    I had one. Each autumn I'd drive mine home
    And he would go back with his to Laios' sheepfold.—   1075
    Is this not true, just as I have described it?

SHEPHERD. True, yes; but it was all so long ago.

MESSENGER. Well, then: do you remember, back in those days,
    That you gave me a baby boy to bring up as my own?

SHEPHERD. What if I did? What are you trying to say?   1080

MESSENGER. King Oedipus was once that little child.

SHEPHERD. Damn you, hold your tongue!

OEDIPUS.   No more of that!
   It is your tongue needs watching, not this man's.

SHEPHERD. My king, my master, what is it I have done wrong?

OEDIPUS. You have not answered his question about the boy.   1085

SHEPHERD. He does not know . . . He is only making trouble . . .

OEDIPUS. Come, speak plainly, or it will go hard with you.

SHEPHERD. In God's name, do not torture an old man!

OEDIPUS. Come here, one of you; bind his arms behind him.

SHEPHERD. Unhappy king! What more do you wish to learn?   1090

OEDIPUS. Did you give this man the child he speaks of?

SHEPHERD.   I did.
    And I would to God I had died that very day.

OEDIPUS. You will die now unless you speak the truth.

SHEPHERD. Yet if I speak the truth, I am worse than dead.

OEDIPUS. (*to* ATTENDANT) He intends to draw it out, apparently— 1095

SHEPHERD. No! I have told you already that I gave him the boy.

OEDIPUS. Where did you get him? From your house? From somewhere
    else?

SHEPHERD. Not from mine, no. A man gave him to me.

OEDIPUS. Is that man here? Whose house did he belong to?

SHEPHERD. For God's love, my king, do not ask me any more!   1100

OEDIPUS. You are a dead man if I have to ask you again.

SHEPHERD. Then . . . Then the child was from the palace of Laios.

OEDIPUS. A slave child? or a child of his own line?

SHEPHERD. Ah, I am on the brink of dreadful speech!

OEDIPUS. And I of dreadful hearing. Yet I must hear.   1105

SHEPHERD. If you must be told, then . . .
    They said it was Laios' child;
  But it is your wife who can tell you about that.

OEDIPUS. My wife!—Did she give it to you?

SHEPHERD.   My lord, she did.

OEDIPUS. Do you know why?

SHEPHERD.   I was told to get rid of it.

OEDIPUS. Oh heartless mother!

SHEPHERD.   But in dread of prophecies . . .   1110

OEDIPUS. Tell me.

SHEPHERD. It was said that the boy would kill his own father.

OEDIPUS. Then why did you give him over to this old man?

SHEPHERD. I pitied the baby, my king,
    And I thought that this man would take him far away
    To his own country.
               He saved him—but for what a fate!   1115
    For if you are what this man says you are,
    No man living is more wretched than Oedipus.

OEDIPUS. Ah God!
    It was true!
        All the prophecies!
            —Now,
    O Light, may I look on you for the last time!   1120
    I, Oedipus,
    Oedipus, damned in his birth, in his marriage damned,
    Damned in the blood he shed with his own hand! (*He
        rushes into the palace.*)

Ode IV

Strophe 1

CHORUS. Alas for the seed of men.
    What measure shall I give these generations   1125
    That breathe on the void and are void
    And exist and do not exist?
    Who bears more weight of joy
    Than mass of sunlight shifting in images,
    Or who shall make his thought stay on   1130
    That down time drifts away?
    Your splendor is all fallen.
    O naked brow of wrath and tears,
    O change of Oedipus!
    I who saw your days call no man blest—   1135
    Your great days like ghosts gone.

Antistrophe 1

    That mind was a strong bow.
    Deep, how deep you drew it then, hard archer,
    At a dim fearful range,
    And brought dear glory down!   1140

You overcame the stranger—
The virgin with her hooking lion claws—
And though death sang, stood like a tower
To make pale Thebes take heart.
Fortress against our sorrow!   1145
True king, giver of laws,
Majestic Oedipus!
No prince in Thebes had ever such renown,
No prince won such grace of power.

Strophe 2

And now of all men ever known   1150
Most pitiful is this man's story:
His fortunes are most changed, his state
Fallen to a low slave's
Ground under bitter fate.
O Oedipus, most royal one!   1155
The great door that expelled you to the light
Gave at night—ah, gave night to your glory:
As to the father, to the fathering son.
All understood too late.
How could that queen whom Laios won,   1160
The garden that he harrowed at his height,
Be silent when that act was done?

Antistrophe 2

But all eyes fail before time's eye,
All actions come to justice there.
Though never willed, though far down the deep past,   1165
Your bed, your dread sirings,
Are brought to book at last.
Child by Laios doomed to die,
Then doomed to lose that fortunate little death,
Would God you never took breath in this air   1170
That with my wailing lips I take to cry:
For I weep the world's outcast.
I was blind, and now I can tell why:
Asleep, for you had given ease of breath
To Thebes, while the false years went by.   1175

Exodos

Enter, from the palace, SECOND MESSENGER.

SECOND MESSENGER. Elders of Thebes, most honored in
      this land,
      What horrors are yours to see and hear, what weight
      Of sorrow to be endured, if, true to your birth,
      You venerate the line of Labdakos!
      I think neither Istros nor Phasis, those great rivers,   1180
      Could purify this place of all the evil
      It shelters now, or soon must bring to light—
      Evil not done unconsciously, but willed.

      The greatest griefs are those we cause ourselves.

CHORAGOS. Surely, friend, we have grief enough already;   1185
      What new sorrow do you mean?

SECOND MESSENGER.   The queen is dead.

CHORAGOS. O miserable queen! But at whose hand?

SECOND MESSENGER.   Her own.
      The full horror of what happened you can not know,
      For you did not see it; but I, who did, will tell you
      As clearly as I can how she met her death.   1190

      When she had left us,
      In passionate silence, passing through the court,
      She ran to her apartment in the house,
      Her hair clutched by the fingers of both hands.
      She closed the doors behind her; then, by that bed   1195
      Where long ago the fatal son was conceived—
      That son who should bring about his father's death—
      We heard her call upon Laios, dead so many years,
      And heard her wail for the double fruit of her marriage,
      A husband by her husband, children by her child.   1200

      Exactly how she died I do not know:
      For Oedipus burst in moaning and would not let us
      Keep vigil to the end: it was by him
      As he stormed about the room that our eyes were caught.
      From one to another of us he went, begging a sword,   1205
      Hunting the wife who was not his wife, the mother

Whose womb had carried his own children and himself.
I do not know: it was none of us aided him,
But surely one of the gods was in control!
For with a dreadful cry   1210
He hurled his weight, as though wrenched out of himself,
At the twin doors: the bolts gave, and he rushed in.
And there we saw her hanging, her body swaying
From the cruel cord she had noosed about her neck.
A great sob broke from him, heartbreaking to hear,   1215
As he loosed the rope and lowered her to the ground.

I would blot out from my mind what happened next!
For the king ripped from her gown the golden brooches
That were her ornament, and raised them, and plunged
   them down
Straight into his own eyeballs, crying, "No more,   1220
No more shall you look on the misery about me,
The horrors of my own doing! Too long you have known
The faces of those whom I should never have seen,
Too long been blind to those for whom I was searching!
From this hour, go in darkness!" And as he spoke,   1225
He struck at his eyes—not once, but many times;
And the blood spattered his beard,
Bursting from his ruined sockets like red hail.

So from the unhappiness of two this evil has sprung,
A curse on the man and woman alike. The old   1230
Happiness of the house of Labdakos
Was happiness enough: where is it today?
It is all wailing and ruin, disgrace, death—all
The misery of mankind that has a name—
And it is wholly and for ever theirs.   1235

CHORAGOS. Is he in agony still? Is there no rest for him?

SECOND MESSENGER. He is calling for someone to open the
         doors wide
      So that all the children of Kadmos may look upon
      His father's murderer, his mother's—no,
      I cannot say it!
                    And then he will leave Thebes,   1240
         Self-exiled, in order that the curse

Which he himself pronounced may depart from the house.
He is weak, and there is none to lead him,
So terrible is his suffering.
                                                 But you will see:
Look, the doors are opening; in a moment   1245
You will see a thing that would crush a heart of stone.

(*The central door is opened;* OEDIPUS, *blinded, is led in.*)

CHORAGOS. Dreadful indeed for men to see.
     Never have my own eyes
     Looked on a sight so full of fear.

     Oedipus!   1250
     What madness came upon you, what daemon
     Leaped on your life with heavier
     Punishment than a mortal man can bear?
     No: I can not even
     Look at you, poor ruined one.   1255
     And I would speak, question, ponder,
     If I were able. No.
     You make me shudder.

OEDIPUS. God. God.
     Is there a sorrow greater?   1260
     Where shall I find harbor in this world?
     My voice is hurled far on a dark wind.
     What has God done to me?

CHORAGOS. Too terrible to think of, or to see.

Strophe 1

OEDIPUS. O cloud of night,   1265
     Never to be turned away: night coming on,
     I can not tell how: night like a shroud!
     My fair winds brought me here.
                                        O God. Again
     The pain of the spikes where I had sight,
     The flooding pain   1270
     Of memory, never to be gouged out.

CHORAGOS. This is not strange.
     You suffer it all twice over, remorse in pain,
     Pain in remorse.

Antistrophe 1

OEDIPUS. Ah dear friend   1275
    Are you faithful even yet, you alone?
    Are you still standing near me, will you stay here,
    Patient, to care for the blind?
                  The blind man!
    Yet even blind I know who it is attends me,
    By the voice's tone—   1280
    Though my new darkness hide the comforter.

CHORAGOS. Oh fearful act!
    What god was it drove you to rake black
    Night across your eyes?

Strophe 2

OEDIPUS. Apollo. Apollo. Dear   1285
    Children, the god was Apollo.
    He brought my sick, sick fate upon me.
    But the blinding hand was my own!
    How could I bear to see
    When all my sight was horror everywhere?   1290

CHORAGOS. Everywhere; that is true.

OEDIPUS. And now what is left?
    Images? Love? A greeting even,
    Sweet to the senses? Is there anything?
    Ah, no, friends: lead me away.   1295
    Lead me away from Thebes.
                Lead the great wreck
    And hell of Oedipus, whom the gods hate.

CHORAGOS. Your misery, you are not blind to that.
    Would God you had never found it out!

Antistrophe 2

OEDIPUS. Death take the man who unbound   1300
    My feet on that hillside
    And delivered me from death to life! What life?
    If only I had died,
    This weight of monstrous doom
    Could not have dragged me and my darlings down.   1305

CHORAGOS. I would have wished the same.

OEDIPUS. Oh never to have come here
        With my father's blood upon me! Never
        To have been the man they call his mother's husband!
        Oh accurst! Oh child of evil,   1310
        To have entered that wretched bed—
                                        the selfsame one!
        More primal than sin itself, this fell to me.

CHORAGOS. I do not know what words to offer you.
        You were better dead than alive and blind.

OEDIPUS. Do not counsel me any more. This punishment   1315
        That I have laid upon myself is just.
        If I had eyes,
        I do not know how I could bear the sight
        Of my father, when I came to the house of Death,
        Or my mother: for I have sinned against them both   1320
        So vilely that I could not make my peace
        By strangling my own life.
                                Or do you think my children,
        Born as they were born, would be sweet to my eyes?
        Ah never, never! Nor this town with its high walls,
        Nor the holy images of the gods.
                                For I,   1325
        Thrice miserable! Oedipus, noblest of all the line
        Of Kadmos, have condemned myself to enjoy
        These things no more, by my own malediction
        Expelling that man whom the gods declared
        To be a defilement in the house of Laios.   1330
        After exposing the rankness of my own guilt,
        How could I look men frankly in the eyes?
        No I swear it,
        If I could have stifled my hearing at its source,
        I would have done it and made all this body   1335
        A tight cell of misery, blank to light and sound:
        So I should have been safe in my dark mind
        Beyond external evil.
                        Ah Kithairon!
        Why did you shelter me? When I was cast upon you,

Why did I not die? Then I should never   1340
Have shown the world my execrable birth.

Ah Polybos! Corinth, city that I believed
The ancient seat of my ancestors: how fair
I seemed, your child! And all the while this evil
Was cancerous within me!
                    For I am sick   1345
In my own being, sick in my origin.

O three roads, dark ravine, woodland and way
Where three roads met: you, drinking my father's blood,
My own blood, spilled by my own hand: can you remember
The unspeakable things I did there, and the things   1350
I went on from there to do?
                    O marriage, marriage!
The act that engendered me, and again the act
Performed by the son in the same bed—
                              Ah, the net
Of incest, mingling fathers, brothers, sons,
With brides, wives, mothers: the last evil   1355
That can be known by men: no tongue can say
How evil!
            No. For the love of God, conceal me
Somewhere far from Thebes; or kill me; or hurl me
Into the sea, away from men's eyes for ever.

Come, lead me, You need not fear to touch me.   1360
Of all men, I alone can bear this guilt.

(*Enter* KREON.)

CHORAGOS. Kreon is here now. As to what you ask,
    He may decide the course to take. He only
    Is left to protect the city in your place.

OEDIPUS. Alas, how can I speak to him? What right have I   1365
    To beg his courtesy whom I have deeply wronged?

KREON. I have not come to mock you, Oedipus,
    Or to reproach you, either.
    (*To* ATTENDANTS) —You, standing there:
    If you have lost all respect for man's dignity,
    At least respect the flame of Lord Helios: 1370
    Do not allow this pollution to show itself

Openly here, an affront to the earth
And Heaven's rain and the light of day. No, take him
Into the house as quickly as you can.
For it is proper   1375
That only the close kindred see his grief.

OEDIPUS. I pray you in God's name, since your courtesy
Ignores my dark expectations, visiting
With mercy this man of all men most execrable:
Give me what I ask—for your good, not for mine.   1380

KREON. And what is it that you turn to me begging for?

OEDIPUS. Drive me out of this country as quickly as may be
To a place where no human voice can ever greet me.

KREON. I should have done that before now—only,
God's will had not been wholly revealed to me.   1385

OEDIPUS. But his command is plain: the parricide
Must be destroyed. I am that evil man.

KREON. That is the sense of it, yes; but as things are,
We had best discover clearly what is to be done.

OEDIPUS. You would learn more about a man like me?   1390

KREON. You are ready now to listen to the god.

OEDIPUS. I will listen. But it is to you
That I must turn for help. I beg you, hear me.
The woman in there—
Give her whatever funeral you think proper: 1395
She is your sister.
                    —But let me go, Kreon!
Let me purge my father's Thebes of the pollution
Of my living here, and go out to the wild hills,
To Kithairon, that has won such fame with me,
The tomb my mother and father appointed for me,   1400
And let me die there, as they willed I should.
And yet I know
Death will not ever come to me through sickness
Or in any natural way: I have been preserved
For some unthinkable fate. But let that be.   1405

As for my sons, you need not care for them.
They are men, they will find some way to live.
But my poor daughters, who have shared my table,
Who never before have been parted from their father—
Take care of them, Kreon; do this for me.   1410

And will you let me touch them with my hands
A last time, and let us weep together?
Be kind, my lord,
Great prince, be kind!
                        Could I but touch them,
They would be mine again, as when I had my eyes.   1415

(*Enter* ANTIGONE *and* ISMENE, *attended.*)

Ah, God!
Is it my dearest children I hear weeping?
Has Kreon pitied me and sent my daughters?

KREON. Yes, Oedipus: I knew that they were dear to you
        In the old days, and know you must love them still.   1420

OEDIPUS. May God bless you for this—and be a friendlier
        Guardian to you than he has been to me!

        Children, where are you?
        Come quickly to my hands: they are your brother's—
        Hands that have brought your father's once clear eyes   1425
        To this way of seeing—
                        Ah dearest ones,
        I had neither sight nor knowledge then, your father
        By the woman who was the source of his own life!
        And I weep for you—having no strength to see you—,
        I weep for you when I think of the bitterness   1430
        That men will visit upon you all your lives.
        What homes, what festivals can you attend
        Without being forced to depart again in tears?
        And when you come to marriageable age,
        Where is the man, my daughters, who would dare   1435
        Risk the bane that lies on all my children?
        Is there any evil wanting? Your father killed
        His father; sowed the womb of her who bore him;

Engendered you at the fount of his own existence!
That is what they will say of you.

                                    Then, whom   1440
Can you ever marry? There are no bridegrooms for you,
And your lives must wither away in sterile dreaming.

O Kreon, son of Menoikeus!
You are the only father my daughters have,
Since we, their parents, are both of us gone for ever.   1445
They are your own blood: you will not let them
Fall into beggary and loneliness;
You will keep them from the miseries that are mine!
Take pity on them; see, they are only children,
Friendless except for you. Promise me this,   1450
Great prince, and give me your hand in token of it.

(KREON *clasps his right hand.*)

Children:
I could say much, if you could understand me,
But as it is, I have only this prayer for you:
Live where you can, be as happy as you can—   1455
Happier, please God, than God has made your father.

KREON. Enough. You have wept enough. Now go within.

OEDIPUS. I must; but it is hard.

KREON.   Time eases all things.

OEDIPUS. You know my mind, then?

KREON.   Say what you desire.

OEDIPUS. Send me from Thebes!

KREON.   God grant that I may!   1460

OEDIPUS. But since God hates me . . .

KREON.   No, he will grant your wish.

OEDIPUS. You promise?

KREON.   I can not speak beyond my knowledge.

OEDIPUS. Then lead me in.

KREON.   Come now, and leave your children.

OEDIPUS. No! Do not take them from me!

KREON.   Think no longer
    That you are in command here, but rather think   1465
    How, when you were, you served your own destruction.

    (*Exeunt into the house all but the* CHORUS; *the* CHORAGOS *chants
    directly to the audience.*)

CHORAGOS. Men of Thebes: look upon Oedipus.
    This the king who solved the famous riddle
    And towered up, most powerful of men.
    No mortal eyes but looked on him with envy,   1470
    Yet in the end ruin swept over him.

    Let every man in mankind's frailty
    Consider his last day; and let none
    Presume on his good fortune until he find
    Life, at his death, a memory without pain.   1475

*Lo*g Entry 1

Questions about your initial responses:

1. (end of Prologue): Write down five words that come to you as
   you think about the Prologue. What questions do you have?

2. (end of Scene I): What words represent your reaction now?
   What questions do you have? What do you predict will happen
   next?

3. (end of Scene II): What questions have been answered for you?
   What additional questions do you have? Was your prediction
   confirmed? What do you think comes next?

4. (end of Scene III): What five words would describe your view
   of Oedipus at this point? What five words would describe
   Iokaste?

5. (end of Scene IV and Exodos): Do you think Oedipus could have
   done anything different to cause a different outcome? What

could he have done, and how would that have changed the outcome? How did the actual outcome compare to your predicted
outcome? What do you think about the fairness of the ending?

*L*og Entry 2

Read or re-read the odes now. After you've read them, respond to
the following questions in your log:

1. What seems to be the purpose of the odes?

2. What themes or patterns can you trace through them?

3. How are they different from the rest of the text?

4. What modern devices (sound, lights, other actors, special effects,
   and so on) fill the roles of the chorus in today's plays and films?

Questioning the Play

After an initial reading of *Oedipus Rex,* you may still have several
questions about the events of the play. Modern readers often want
to know why Iokaste would marry someone young enough to be
her son or why she did not notice the scars on Oedipus's ankles.
What do you wonder about?

In presenting a concept through the actions of characters, Sophocles
has omitted details that were not essential to his idea. His decision
leaves gaps in the story that modern readers want filled. Filling those
gaps is an act of interpretation, just as responding to the actual words
and performance of the play is. Your wondering and the answers you
supply offer additional angles of vision for understanding the play.

*L*og Entry 3

Before you read the play a second time, list several details that you
wonder about. As you re-read, cross off those details that Sophocles
reveals. After your second reading of the play, read the poems at the

end of the chapter to see how current poets deal with gaps that they identify. Be cautious, though. Don't think that the modern poets are telling us about the characters as Sophocles conceived of them. Remember that these are modern transformations, not to be taken as the rest of the story that Sophocles knew but omitted. There are suggestions at the end of the chapter for ways in which you might want to deal creatively with one or more of the details that remain on your list.

Performance

Although it may be an unusual practice for those of us who are worried about doing as much as possible in too little time, a second reading of certain works of literature often leads to greater understanding of the text. As a performer/director, you should re-read the entire play, looking for the subtext, the other nine-tenths of the iceberg, that Sophocles does not state explicitly. You have two large questions to answer: What might have been Sophocles' purpose in presenting the traditional story in the way he did in this play, and what emotions would you like an audience to feel as they view the play today? As you explore Sophocles' purpose, you also explore some of the decisions he must have made in writing the play. Why, for example, does he continue the play beyond Oedipus's realization and blinding? Some critics suggest it should have ended there. And, as you think about the emotions you would like to create in a contemporary audience, you must make your own decisions about the ways the subtext can be used to accomplish your purposes.

Collaborating

In a group of three to five, discuss the following questions after re-reading the play.

- What are some of the implications of Sophocles' use of the imagery of blindness and insight? How does he use them ironically? What are other uses of irony in the play?

- The play is something of a detective story but with a twist—the detective is also the criminal he seeks. To us it may seem odd that the truth dawns on other people before it does on Oedipus. What effect does Sophocles achieve by revealing the truth in the way that he does?

- How does Kreon feel toward Oedipus? What values does he represent? Do his feelings change during the play? In what ways might Kreon be adversely or positively affected by the revelations at the end?

- What single line contains one of the themes of the play? Why do you think so?

*Pe*rformance

Put your increased understanding of the play to work now. By performing one segment of *Oedipus Rex,* you can reveal the subtext, present your interpretation to others, and, in the process, enlarge your concept of the play.

- Select one small part of the play to perform. Select a significant segment; it may represent a theme, reveal the nature of one or two characters, or advance the plot through an important conflict or through the revelation of an important piece of information.

- Find other people to take the parts in your segment—in most cases, you will need only one or two others. Together examine the segment for ways to reveal the print message through non-print means: pacing, tone, emphasis, silence, and blocking.

- After you have spent some time preparing, you will present your segment for the class. Don't worry if another group selects the same segment—that provides an excellent opportunity to discuss the ways different directors present a play.

- If you have plenty of time, you may want to memorize your lines. If you do not memorize your speeches, though, be sure to practice them frequently so you need not rely on the script the whole time. In fact, the performance will look better if you put your lines on small notecards instead of carrying the entire book to the front of the room.

Log Entry 4

Considering the following questions may help you plan your performance.

- What is significant about the segment you have chosen?

- What is the relationship between (or among) the characters? How will you show this relationship?

- Where will the characters move during the segment? Draw a floor plan to record your ideas.

- What has occurred earlier in the play that affects this segment?

- In presenting your segment, will you modernize it or will you stay with the traditional form?

- What are the most important words and phrases in this segment? How will you indicate those?

- If there is a conflict in your segment, how will you play that?

- How will you deal with irony if it exists in your segment?

If you can make copies of your segment, you can mark on those, recording your decisions. If not, you could use sticky notes in the margins of the textbook.

Transforming *Oedipus Rex*

Linda Yee was a high school student in California when she wrote "Oedipus in Exile." Her poem is based on metaphors that she created for Oedipus as she strove for a fuller understanding of his character. Metaphors are useful tools for transformations, as you learned in

Chapter 2, because they enlarge our view of a character. As you read the poem silently first, then aloud, think about the additional interpretations you gain through the metaphors and the mood that Yee creates.

Oedipus in Exile
Linda Yee

A dolphin's low moan
Echoes in the night.
The sound, like tidal waves
That bash against jagged cliffs,
Irritates the ears
Of suppliants
Who must not hear.

The slick blue fish
Tangles in the meshy trap, is
Plucked from the water.
The grey, still air suffocates.
He twists, wavers back and forth,
Then delivers a
Single acrid cry
Above the tuna's
Floundering splashes.

The brilliant, burning sun
Scorches his eyes.
He can only listen
To the crystal chimes
Of a distant buoy.
They arouse shadows
Of a bright, purple past.

Once, in a dream,
He was a bull,
With horns as swift and sharp
As a diamond's edge.
His head, a flickering ember,
A brute, "whom all . . . call the great,"
Stands as stout as an oak tree
Ready to crush
Commoner or king.

The gates snap open.
He shoots into the ring.
Loud screams muffle his ears.
Run, capture the waving red cloak.
Horns lunge forward
For the kill.

It's gone. He stumbles
And flinches.
A sword grates
Through his eyeballs.

A wave rushes back
Up on shore
and falls
Again and again.
The pain's bitter resonance:
Prickly pine tree thorns
Pinching at the eyes and joints.

This poem can give us a fuller view of Oedipus. But what about Iokaste? What did Sophocles tell us about her as a wife, mother, or woman? What is her role in the downfall of Oedipus? Ruth Eisenberg, a drama teacher in New York state, was curious about what Sophocles did not include. In fact, she became so intrigued by this one character that she wrote a poem giving Iokaste's version of the story. That poem, along with Eisenberg's explanation of her writing process, may fill in some of the details that you wondered about. Eisenberg uses a traditional English spelling when she writes of "Jocasta."

Jocasta
Ruth Eisenberg

I

When she learned the king's power,
Jocasta lost delight in being queen.
Laius was a cold, dry man. Looking at him
brought the image of her baby, his feet
pierced and bound, her baby left to die
on the mountain slope. They would
have no other children.

I remember Laius drunk that night, crying
for Chrysippus, the source of his curse.
Wanting his boy, he took me instead
and threw me on my back to have his way.
I am fifteen and afraid to resist
and tell myself it is my husband's right;
the gods decree a wife obey her spouse.

Sober, Laius recalls Apollo's threat:
our son will kill him, beget upon me.
Nine months drag like oxen ploughing.
With icy eyes Laius watches me swell.
I fear the gods and beg Hera for a girl,
but as foretold, I give birth to a son.
Laius takes the child to bind its feet.
The baby cries, and Laius turns away.
He summons a servant and orders me to hand
my baby over, threatening me when I cry.
The king will keep his own hands clean.

At the public altar, Laius
offered bulls and lambs in ritual
slaughter. The everburning fire raged
so the offerings charred, and Jocasta
trembled at the gods' displeasure.

Upon the gates this dawn, a strange creature
appeared and woke all Thebes. In raucous voice
she cried, "A riddle. Who'll solve my riddle?"
At first our people came to gawk, then marvel.
Some trembled, children hid their heads and cried.
I've heard old tales the minstrels sing of her,
and never did expect to live to see
a Sphinx—part woman, bird, and lion too . . .
And what she asks is strange as well: four legs,
then two, then three. What can it be? No one
knows the answer. No one.

The Sphinx brought pestilence and
drought. Rivers and streams ran dry, vines
shriveled. But until her riddle was solved,

the creature would not leave. On the gates
she sat, her destructive song echoing
from empty wells.

> My life is a toad. All day and all night
> the Sphinx. We cannot escape her song.
> Song! More like wail or whine or scream.
> Laius is useless as always. Deceitful
> man, I hate him, hate his touch.

> The land is parched; flocks die. Our people
> haggard, starving, plead to ease their distress.
> What can we do? Mortals cannot make the rain.
> I suggest Laius seek Apollo's help.
> To get away, he welcomes the idea to go
> to Delphi and proclaims a pilgrimage.

On the sunswept road to Delphi,
Laius was killed. The servant reporting
the death begged Jocasta to let him tend
flocks in the hills. Sending him on his way,
she shut herself in the palace.

> The prophecy was false. If gods control
> all things, how can that be? For surely chance
> does not . . . No, no. Yet Laius killed our son
> and not the other way. That sin diseased
> his soul. I bless the gods that I,
> at last, am free.

> I dream of my baby night after night.
> He is dancing for the gods with bound feet.
> I do not understand how he can dance so.
> When he jumps, he trips, falling in a heap.
> The gods just laugh and turn away to drink.
> I sit ravelling knots. The knots become rope.
> I wake shaking and muffle my tears in the sheets.

II

"Man" answered the young stranger
whose red hair caught the sun's rays,
and the riddle was solved. True to her

promise, the Sphinx dashed herself to
death. Thebes was free.

  Hailing their hero, the people
elected Oedipus king. Gratefully,
he accepted the rule and with it the hand
of Thebes' queen, Jocasta.

    I see young Oedipus in radiant
    sunlight, Apollo blinding me to all
    but young and vital strength. Deep in myself
    I feel a pulsebeat, something asleep
    begins to wake, as though a dormant seed
    sends up a shoot, opens a leaf. That's how
    Aphrodite touches me. I love this youth.
    My sun, I rise to him and rise with him.

  From a land of rock and misery, Thebes
became a bower. Brilliant poppies
dotted the land. The wells filled, crops
flourished, and the flocks grew fat again.

  Before the people's eyes, Jocasta
became young. Her dark hair gleamed, her
eye was bright and her laughter cheered
the halls of the palace.

    Oedipus has become my Apollo warming
    my days and nights. I am eighteen again
    with poppies in my hair. I am the poppies,
    bright little blooms with milk in them.
    Like them, I seem to spring from rocky ground.
    Like their color and his hair, our love flames.

    Sweet Aphrodite, you rush through me, a stream
    until you burst like foam that crests the sea.
    Your blessing washes what was once a barren
    ground. I walk among the roses, feel
    your blush upon my cheeks. Oh lovely goddess,
    I send you swans and doves.

  Thebes prospered these years:
the gnarled olive bent lower with fruit.
Lambs frisked in the fields and pipers'

songs rang through the hills. Jocasta had
four children. Psalms of joy were sung
and danced for the gods.

> With four children, the hours run away.
> Their hunger, games and tears take all my time.
> In bed, with Oedipus, I sleep in peace.
> He was at first my headstrong bull, but now
> he is what a man, a king, should be.

> I like to see him walking in the yard,
> his stiff, funny gait, his hair burnished
> by Apollo's brilliant rays.

> Mine turns gray but he doesn't seem to mind.
> Our love has brought to me the joy I missed
> when I was young and thought I'd never know.

> At last, I lay to rest my little boy,
> his shadow vanished now from all my dreams.

III

Years of plenty at an end, Thebes
was inflicted with drought. The earth
burned as crops withered, cattle and
sheep sickened.

> While days were once too short, now each one drags
> a slow furrow, the earth heavy with heat,
> lament and prayer. When I go to the fields
> the women clutch my gown and plead my help.
> Too many children sicken. The healthy droop.
> At home, the girls sit listless, my sons tangle
> while Oedipus complains his ankles twinge.
> He limps and growls just like a wounded pup.

Jocasta, very gray now, walked
with a more measured step. More than
a loving wife, she was also counselor
to Oedipus.

> Blaming himself because the land is parched,
> Oedipus frets, alarmed he's failed the gods

somehow, that they are punishing Thebes.
In turn I pray, lighting fire after fire,
but none burns true. I call on Aphrodite
and offer her doves, but they flap their wings
and peck each others' eyes. When I ask Apollo
to dim his eye, his answer scalds.

No relief at hand, Oedipus sought
aid from Delphi. The report came back
a confusing riddle about Laius' death.
Suspecting treason, Oedipus feared
conspiracy against his own throne.

Oedipus needs someone to blame. He calls
Creon traitor, Tiresias false seer.
I take him in my arms and stroke his hair.
He tells me what Tiresias has foreseen.

I laugh and tell him I too once believed
that prophecy controlled our lives, that seers
had magic vision the rest of us did not.
I tell the story of Laius, how it
was foretold he would die at his son's hand
and how that baby died when one week old.

As I speak I feel so strange, as though my tale
came from another life about someone else.

My words do not comfort, they flame new fears.
He relates what drove him from home, tales that he
would kill his father and bring rank fruit
from his mother's womb. He fears he has
been cursed. Dear gods, how can I comfort him?

IV

From Corinth, a messenger
brought news of Polybus' death,
the king whom Oedipus called father.

You say that Polybus is dead. Dare I
greet death with joy? Can that be blasphemy?
My heart flies into song: His father's dead—
my Oedipus lives safe. His prophecy

is false. Is false as Laius' was. Oh bless
your fate, dear love. You need no longer fear.

Corinth wished Oedipus to return
and rule. Fearing he would sleep with
his mother, Oedipus refused. Nothing
to fear, the messenger assured. Merope
was a barren woman.

Jocasta began to tremble. Her hands
rose to cover her mouth.

What's this? What's this? What words do I hear?
How can I shut his silly mouth, tell him
Go. Leave. We will not heed your words.
My tongue stops, rooted in my mouth.
I look at Oedipus. He does not see
me watching him. His face is strained, his eyes
are glaring blue. I try to stop the questions.
"Oedipus, I beg you, do not hear this out."

When Oedipus insisted, the
messenger told the story of the king's
infancy—how he, a shepherd then,
had helped to save the king's life
when a baby, a baby with bound feet.

Oh God. Oh cold, gold God. Apollo,
you chill me. My mind is ice, and I hear
my mouth say freezing words to Oedipus.
To my husband. My son. "God keep you from
the knowledge of who you are. Unhappy,
Oedipus, my poor, damned Oedipus,
that is all I can call you, and the last thing
I shall ever call you."

V

Her face ashen, Jocasta rushed
into the palace, her hands showing her
the way to her own quarters. She
ordered the guards to let no one in.
Ignoring all offers of help, she commanded
her women to leave her alone.

I can't believe. I can't believe. Oh God,
He is my son. I've loved my son but not
as mothers should, but in my bed, in me.
All that I loved the most, his youth that made
our love the summer sun, wrong, all wrong.
Vile. He caressed me here and here. And I
returned his touch. Odious hands. My flesh
crawls with worms.

My god, we've had four children.

In her chamber, she looked at her
bed, sat on it, then jumped up as though
stung. Covering her eyes with her hands,
she shook her head back and forth, again
and again, her body rocking.

Oh, Oedipus, what good was our love if
it comes only to shame? To children whom
all Thebes can curse? Such children, even ours,
are rightly damned.

Although we could not know who we were
and loved in innocence, still we are monsters
in the eyes of god and man. Our names will mean
disgrace and guilt forever.

Walking to her dressing table,
she stood before it picking up small
objects: combs, a gold box, a pair of
brooches. Noticing a bracelet given her
by her father when she was a bride,
she let forth a dreadful groan.

Oh Laius, Laius, you brought this on me.
My fate was sealed my wedding day. Chrysippus
was innocent as I; for you this curse
was uttered, a curse that falls on me. Oh,
that I must bear the shame, that I must be
destroyed by your corruption. And our son,
because you sinned, is ruined, damned.

My marriage day . . . what choices did I have?
As many as the night you came to me.

The only choice a woman has is that she wed
accepting what the gods and men decree.
It is not just. It never can be right.

Moving decisively, she walked to the
doors and bolted them, straining against
their heavy weight. The women on the other
side called to her, but again she bade them
go away.

Falling on her knees, she pummeled
her stomach as though to punish her
womb. As she did, she called her children's names, one name, Oedipus, again
and again.

I thought him buried, forgotten. But no,
for countless days and nights these many years
he's thrust himself on me instead. My bed
once stained with birthing blood is now forever
stained; what once was love become a rank
corruption.

Rising painfully, sore, she turned
to the small altar in her chamber.
Smashing a jar which held incense, she
began in a voice of char to call on
Apollo and Aphrodite.

As she raised her eyes, she raised
her fist and shook it against
the silent air.

Apollo, you blinded me to his scars,
his age, any resemblance to Laius.
And you, Aphrodite, cruel sister of the sun,
set my woman's body afire, matching my
ripe years and hungers with his youth and strength.
Paralyzing my mind, you inflamed my heart.

The years I prayed to you and praised you
were all charade. You so enjoyed my dance.
We are your fools to trifle with, your joke.

We tremble to question what the future holds.
As though it matters, we think asking spoils
our luck. But your injustice mocks all hope.

I hear a chant pounding inside my head.
Five babies. Five abominations.
As though a chorus raises call to prayer.
Five babies. Five abominations.

No call to prayer. It is a call to curse
the gods. No longer will I be their fool.

From her robe, she removed her
braided belt. As she looped its strands,
she heard, from the courtyard, a man's
voice scream in anguish. Undeflected, she
tied the necessary knots, slipping the loop
back and forth. Satisfied, she settled
the noose around her neck.

Five babies cursed by heavenly whim,
cursed in their lives without chance or hope.
Mothers ought not to love their children so.

Gathering up her skirts, she climbed
up on the stool.

And wives be more than merely bedside pawns.
Those who cannot shape their lives are better
dead.

She stepped onto the air.

Ruth Eisenberg, author of "Jocasta," speaks about her process of
writing and revising the poem:

I needed to hear the poem. For me poetry is a spoken art, and as I
write I always say the lines out loud. But to hear the poem in a voice
other than mine, to hear the responses of others to the lines, would
be, I knew, a great help. When it happened, interestingly enough,
three women read the poem. My imaginative director friend, Joan
Thorne, saw Jocasta as three women in one: the innocent, the queen,
and the wife-mother. She also saw the five sections in two different

ways: first as musical themes, and secondly as a progressive movement towards a woman's interior life.

The reading revealed weaknesses in Sections III and IV. They were
the least dramatically alive: the most narrative, most derivative, and
the least felt. At this revelation I became aware of how intimidated I
was by the play. How dare I to have trespassed on sacred ground?
For me *Oedipus Rex* is the greatest play ever written. How could I
challenge Sophocles on his own turf?

Then I realized I wasn't challenging him, that my turf and his
were different. He was concerned with Oedipus. Jocasta's lines were
for his reaction; she was his foil, and in her recognition scene, his
antagonist. Sophocles didn't even give her many lines in that scene.
Therefore, anything I had added didn't challenge him; rather, I had
accepted an opportunity to fill in the blanks. I added new verses in
her voice. Jocasta goes through an absolute roller coaster of feeling
when she hears the words of the messenger from Corinth, from a
sense of false reassurance to horror. She tries to protect Oedipus from
the knowledge (he, if you recall, turns on her and mistakes her mo-
tive) and stands not just awed but appalled at the work of the gods.

*Co*llaborating

Using both poems, the play, your own scenes, and the interpretations of others in your class, think about the following questions.
Discuss them with a small group of three to five.

- How would you describe the central characters of the play now?
  What are their hopes, their fears, their motivations?

- How do the later transformations in poetry shape your view of
  Sophocles' theme? If Sophocles wanted to present the idea that
  we cannot control everything because we cannot know everything, how does either of the subsequent poems add light to his
  theme? If Sophocles wanted people to see what happened when
  someone tried to defy the power of the gods, how does either
  poem contribute to that theme?

- Is there any relevance for modern viewers of the story of *Oedipus
  Rex* as told by Sophocles? If so, do the poems increase or detract
  from the relevance you identify?

Building Your Course Portfolio

Select one or more of the following options to complete as portfolio entries. Your poem, essay, or video should demonstrate your understanding of how performing a text can transform it from words on a page into living people working out meaningful issues. Your portfolio entry should also represent your abilities to comprehend drama and to compose your thoughts effectively.

Save these entries to include in your final course portfolio.

Portfolio Entry

- Read what critics have said about this play. Then do a persuasive essay or speech showing where you disagree with one of the critics and give reasons for your opinion.

- One motif that some people have identified in the play is duality—two apparently opposite terms that exist together, creating dramatic tension. Make a three-column chart, identifying dual elements and indicating their impact on the plot, characterizations, or themes of the play. Your columns would be labeled, from left to right: "first term," "opposite term," "impact." For example, in *Oedipus Rex* you might have:

First Term	Opposite Term	Impact
sight	blindness	Although he is blind, Teiresias is the only person who can "see" the entire truth—irony heightens characterization of Oedipus's "blindness"

Then write an essay about the effects of duality on your understanding of the play.

- Find another play to read, and select a segment to perform, ana-lyzing it as you did in this chapter. The play could be any style; it need not be Greek. Include a videotape of the performance, along with all of your performance notes, for your portfolio.

- Write a poem or a scene that fills in one of the gaps in a play that you select. For example, if you choose *Oedipus Rex,* you might reinterpret Iokaste or turn part of Eisenberg's poem into a scene for a different version of the play. You could also show Kreon talking with Teiresias about Oedipus's puzzling behavior.

6

Death and
Transformation

*I*n Chapter 1, we asked you to look at a poem from seven angles of vision. These angles, in one way or another, have formed the basis for the reading and writing activities we have suggested throughout this book. We now ask you to work through all seven angles as you read and study an essay written by Annie Dillard. Reading an essay requires essentially the same processes as reading a poem. However, it often seems different because of the special demands of the essay as well as our own different purposes for reading this kind of writing.

*A*ngles of Vision on an Essay

Although the word *literature* generally evokes the idea of poems, stories, novels, and plays, it also includes that very large category we call the *essay*. An essay may be interpretive, persuasive, or argumentative; it may be speculative, meditative, or reflective. Annie Dillard's essay "Death of a Moth" falls into this latter category, but it contains a great deal of close observation as well.

As you read, use a double-entry log to note ideas that you find provocative, or jot down questions or ideas that relate to your experiences. Making quick drawings or sketches is a good way to register your response. Record words or phrases that you like or that you want to go back to later. Don't be too analytical on your first reading; read the essay with an eye toward making connections, or just to get the overall sense. You may find it helpful to reread the essay several times as you did the poem in Chapter 1. We hope that you will do so.

Death of a Moth
Annie Dillard

I live on northern Puget Sound, in Washington state, alone. I have a gold cat, who sleeps on my legs, named Small. In the morning I joke to her blank face, Do you remember last night? Do you remember? I throw her out before breakfast, so I can eat.

There is a spider, too, in the bathroom, with whom I keep a sort of company. Her little outfit always reminds me of a certain moth I helped to kill. The spider herself is of uncertain lineage, bulbous at the abdomen and drab. Her six-inch mess of a web works, works somehow, works miraculously, to keep her alive and me amazed. The web itself is in a corner behind the toilet, connecting tile wall to tile wall and floor, in a place where there is, I would have thought, scant traffic. Yet under the web are sixteen or so corpses she has tossed to the floor.

The corpses appear to be mostly sow bugs, those little armadillo creatures who like to travel flat out in houses, and die round. There is also a new shred of earwig, three old spider skins crinkled and clenched, and two moth bodies, wingless and huge and empty, moth bodies I drop to my knees to see.

Today the earwig shines darkly and gleams, what there is of him: a dorsal curve of thorax and abdomen, and a smooth pair of cerci[1] by which I knew his name. Next week, if the other bodies are any indication, he will be shrunken and gray, webbed to the floor with dust. The sow bugs beside him are hollow and empty of color, fragile, a breath away from brittle fluff. The spider skins lie on their sides, translucent and ragged, their legs drying in knots. And the moths, the empty moths, stagger against each other, headless, in a confusion of arching strips of chitin like peeling varnish, like a jumble of buttresses for cathedral domes, like nothing resembling moths, so that I should hesitate to call them moths, except that I have had some experience with the figure Moth reduced to a nub.

Two summers ago I was camping alone in the Blue Ridge Mountains in Virginia. I had hauled myself and gear up there to read, among other things, James Ramsey Ullman's *The Day on Fire,* a novel about Rimbaud that had made me want to be a writer when I was sixteen;[2] I was hoping it would do it again. So I read, lost, every day sitting under a tree by my tent, while warblers swung in the leaves overhead and bristle worms trailed their inches over the twiggy dirt at my feet; and I read every night by candlelight, while barred owls called in the forest and pale moths massed round my head in the clearing, where my light made a ring.

Moths kept flying into the candle. They would hiss and recoil, lost upside down in the shadows among my cooking pans. Or they would

---

[1] Plural of cercus, posterior feeler of an insect.
[2] French poet Arthur Rimbaud (1854–1891) himself began writing at age sixteen and produced his major work before he was twenty. Ullman's novel was published in 1958.

singe their wings and fall, and their hot wings, as if melted, would stick to the first thing they touched—a pan, a lid, a spoon—so that the snagged moths could flutter only in tiny arcs, unable to struggle free. These I could release by a quick flip with a stick; in the morning I would find my cooking stuff gilded with torn flecks of moth wings, triangles of shiny dust here and there on the aluminum. So I read, and boiled water, and replenished candles, and read on.

One night a moth flew into the candle, was caught, burnt dry and held. I must have been staring at the candle, or maybe I looked up when a shadow crossed my page; at any rate, I saw it all. A golden female moth, a biggish one with a two-inch wingspan, flapped into the firs, dropped her abdomen into the wet wax, stuck, flamed, frazzled and fried in a second. Her moving wings ignited like tissue paper, enlarging the circle of light in the clearing and creating out of the darkness the sudden blue sleeves of my sweater, the green leaves of jewelweed by my side, the ragged red trunk of a pine. At once the light contracted again and the moth's wings vanished in a fine, foul smoke. At the same time her six legs clawed, curled, blackened, and ceased, disappearing utterly. And her head jerked in spasms, making a spattering noise; her antennae crisped and burned away and her heaving mouth parts crackled like pistol fire. When it was all over, her head was, so far as I could determine, gone, gone the long way of her wings and legs. Had she been new, or old? Had she mated and laid her eggs, had she done her work? All that was left was the glowing horn shell of her abdomen and thorax—a fraying, partially collapsed gold tube jammed upright in the candle's round pool.

And then this moth-essence, this spectacular skeleton, began to act as a wick. She kept burning. The wax rose in the moth's body from her soaking abdomen to her thorax to the jagged hole where her head should be, and widened into a flame, a saffron-yellow flame that robed her to the ground like any immolating monk. That candle had two wicks, two flames of identical height, side by side. The moth's head was fire. She burned for two hours, until I blew her out.

She burned for two hours without changing, without bending or leaning—only glowing within, like a building fire glimpsed through silhouetted walls, like a hollow saint, like a flame-faced virgin gone to God, while I read by her light, kindled, while Rimbaud in Paris burnt out his brains in a thousand poems, while night pooled wetly at my feet.

And that is why I believe those hollow crisps on the bathroom floor are moths. I think I know moths, and fragments of moths and chips and tatters of utterly empty moths, in any state. How many of you, I asked the people in my class, which of you want to give your lives and be writers? I was trembling from coffee, or cigarettes, or the closeness of faces all around me. (Is this what we live for? I thought; is this the only final beauty: the color of any skin in any light, and living, human eyes?) All hands rose to the question. (You, Nick? Will you? Margaret? Randy? Why do I want them to mean it?) And then I tried to tell them what the choice must mean: you can't be anything else. You must go at your life with a broadax. . . . They had no idea what I was saying. (I have two hands, don't I? And all this energy, for as long as I can remember. I'll do it in the evenings, after skiing, or on the way home from the bank, or after the children are asleep. . . .) They thought I was raving again. It's just as well.

I have three candles here on the table which I disentangle from the plants and light when visitors come. Small usually avoids them, although once she came too close and her tail caught fire; I rubbed it out before she noticed. The flames move light over everyone's skin, draw light to the surface of the faces of my friends. When the people leave I never blow the candles out, and after I'm asleep they flame and burn.

Angle 1: Initial Response

Log Entry 1

Read through the double-entry log you created as you read "Death of a Moth," and review your initial impressions. As Log Entry 1, make a summary statement about your first impressions of this essay.

Angle 2: Story Threads

One of the ways we construct meaning as we read is to try to find connections between what is in the text and what is in our own lives. Dillard begins "Death of a Moth" in a very down-to-earth way, describing in minute detail the spider that lives in her bathroom and the corpses that litter the area beneath its web. It isn't until the second paragraph that she turns to the narrative of the moth.

Recall an observation of something small, or think of an occasion when you became absorbed in watching something very small, something alive. Go back to that time in your mind and recreate the scene. What were you doing at the time? What caught your attention? What actually happened? What thoughts did the observation trigger? Why do you think you have remembered it?

*Lo*g Entry 2

Record your recollected observations in close detail. Include a sketch of what you saw. Make any connections you can between your own observations and Dillard's in "Death of a Moth."

Angle 3: Shifting Perspectives

In the last two paragraphs, Dillard refers to the people in her writing class. "They had no idea what I was saying," she writes. Imagine that you are in her class. You have listened to her talking about the moth that flew into the candle. She has used a lot of religious words and phrases, like "immolating monk" and "flamefaced virgin." You've just heard her say, "You must go at your life with a broadax." What is she talking about?

*Lo*g Entry 3

Write an account of this class session with Dillard. Choose one of the following options for your account or make up your own scenario.

- Answer the question: What is she talking about?

- Write up your observations of the class for a friend who was sick and unable to attend class that day.

- Write a response to Dillard's remarks to hand in as your next assignment for the class.

Another way to shift perspectives when looking at a piece from different angles is to consider the title; what if this essay were to have a different title? Select alternative titles and indicate their implications in your log. Label this Log Entry 3A.

Collaborating

Share your ideas with other members of your group. Talk about the similarities and differences in how each of you perceived what Dillard said in the hypothetical class. Compare the alternative titles you gave this essay, explaining your reasons for selecting them.

Angle 4: Connecting with the Writer

It is often useful to know something about the background of an essayist. Annie Dillard's most famous work is her first book, *Pilgrim at Tinker Creek,* a book of personal, reflective essays stemming from the very close observations of a small creek that ran behind her house. That book won her many readers and the Pulitzer Prize. She has also written a novel, a book of poems, other collections of essays, a book of literary theory, and an autobiography, *An American Childhood.* In reading "Death of a Moth," you learn something about Dillard's approach to writing as well as to life.

*Lo*g Entry 4

Imagine that you were to interview Ms. Dillard about how she came to write the moth essay. What kinds of questions would you ask? How do you think she would respond? Use your own experiences of observing something in nature and any clues you might have from this essay to make up your response.

Angle 5: Language and Craft

*Lo*g Entry 5

One angle of vision that helps us get an overall picture of a complex work—essay, poem, or story—is a map. For this essay, construct a map that shows how the essay is developed. You may work with one partner and use any organizational pattern you find workable. You might begin by figuring out what you see as the central image or primary idea. (There is no right answer to this activity; you decide and then substantiate your decision with appropriate quotations.) Spider webs would be one appropriate organizational metaphor; think of others. Use images, symbols, sketches, and drawings as they illustrate your concept of the whole essay— organization and ideas.

*Co*llaborating

Put your graphics on the board and use them as a basis for a class discussion of this essay by Annie Dillard.

Angle 6: Recasting the Text

*Lo*g Entry 6

Dillard herself, as you know, wrote both poetry and prose. There are a lot of poems hidden in this essay. Select an image or an idea that you find provocative and read through the essay recording words and phrases that pertain to the subject you have chosen. Then recast the essay into a poem or a sequence of poems. Don't try to include everything. Focus on only one image or idea for each poem you try, but limit yourself basically to Dillard's words. Think of it as a puzzle, and try to construct a meaningful poem. Give it a title, but again, choose words for the title that you find somewhere in the essay. Share your first drafts and help each other refine your poems. Here is a sample from Fran Claggett's log.

Reading a Novel About Rimbaud
Fran Claggett

I think I know moths,
the flames that move light
the color of skin.

Gold cat,
barred owl,
a spider: moth-essence.

Is this what we live for?
Is this the only final beauty?

Angle 7: You, the Text, the World

As we've emphasized throughout this book, it is important to know that you do not need to come to a conclusion about the meaning of a work of literature. You may need to form your ideas about the meaning a work has for you at a particular moment, when you are asked to write an interpretive or analytic essay, for example. Another day, however, when you are in a different mood or have had an experience that relates to the events in the work, you may find your understanding or envisionment of the text has changed.

Every step you take toward creating richer meaning involves changing perspectives, making connections, and facing new possibilities. You make interpretive decisions each time you look through a different lens. By looking at a work from different angles, your reading becomes more imaginative, intellectual, and emotional.

As a way of providing a richer context for your reading of Dillard's piece, we're including a final piece, "The Death of the Moth," a very well-known essay by Virginia Woolf, one of the most distinguished and influential writers of the early twentieth century. Those familiar with the Woolf essay might wonder whether it was in some way responsible for Dillard's attention as she observed and later wrote about her encounter with the death of a moth—whether Dillard's essay was in a sense a recasting of Woolf's.

The Death of the Moth

Virginia Woolf

Moths that fly by day are not properly to be called moths; they do not excite that pleasant sense of dark autumn nights and ivy-blossom which the commonest yellow underwing asleep in the shadow of the curtain never fails to rouse in us. They are hybrid creatures, neither gay like butterflies nor somber like their own species. Nevertheless the present specimen, with his narrow hay-coloured wings, fringed with a tassel of the same colour, seemed to be content with life. It was a pleasant morning, mid-September, mild, benignant, yet with a keener breath than that of the summer months. The plough was already scoring the field opposite the window, and where the share had been, the earth was pressed flat and gleamed with moisture. Such vigour came rolling in from the fields and the down beyond that it was difficult to keep the eyes strictly turned upon the book. The rooks too were keeping one of their annual festivities; soaring round the tree-tops until it looked as if a vast net with thousands of black knots in it has been cast up into the air; which, after a few moments sank slowly down upon the trees until every twig seemed to have a knot at the end of it. Then, suddenly, the net would be thrown into the air again in a wider circle this time, with the utmost clamour and vociferation, as though to be thrown into the air and settle slowly down upon the tree-tops were a tremendously exciting experience.

The same energy which inspired the rooks, the ploughmen, the horses, and even, it seemed, the lean bare-backed downs, sent the moth fluttering from side to side of his square of the window-pane. One could not help watching him. One was, indeed, conscious of a queer feeling of pity for him. The possibilities of pleasure seemed that morning so enormous and so various that to have only a moth's part in life, and a day moth's at that, appeared a hard fate, and his zest in enjoying his meagre opportunities to the full, pathetic. He flew vigorously to one corner of his compartment, and, after waiting there a second, flew across to the other. What remained for him but to fly to a third corner and then to a fourth? That was all he could do, in spite of the size of the down, the width of the sky, the far-off smoke of houses, and the romantic voice, now and then, of a steamer out at sea. What he could do he did. Watching him, it seemed as if a fiber, very thin but pure, of the enormous energy of the world had been thrust into his frail and diminutive body. As often as he crossed the pane, I could fancy that a thread of vital light became visible. He was little or nothing but life.

Yet, because he was so small, and so simple a form of the energy that was rolling in at the open window and driving its way through so many narrow and intricate corridors in my own brain and in those of other human beings, there was something marvelous as well as pathetic about him. It was as if someone had taken a tiny bead of pure life and decking it as lightly as possible with down and feathers, had set it dancing and zigzagging to show us the true nature of life. Thus displayed one could not get over the strangeness of it. One is apt to forget all about life, seeing it humped and bossed and garnished and cumbered so that it has to move with the greatest circumspection and dignity. Again, the thought of all that life might have been had he been born in any other shape caused one to view his simple activities with a kind of pity.

After a time, tired by his dancing apparently, he settled on the window ledge in the sun, and the queer spectacle being at an end, I forgot about him. Then, looking up, my eye was caught by him. He was trying to resume his dancing, but seemed either so stiff or so awkward that he could only flutter to the bottom of the window-pane; and when he tried to fly across it he failed. Being intent on other matters I watched these futile attempts for a time without thinking, unconsciously waiting for him to resume his flight, as one waits for a machine that has stopped momentarily to start again, without considering the reason for its failure. After perhaps a seventh attempt he slipped from the wooden ledge and fell, fluttering his wings, on to his back on the window-sill. That helplessness of his attitude roused me. It flashed upon me that he was in difficulties; he could no longer raise himself; his legs struggled vainly. But, as I stretched out a pencil, meaning to help him to right himself, it came over me that the failure and awkwardness were the approach of death. I laid the pencil down again.

The legs agitated themselves once more. I looked as if for the enemy against which he struggled. I looked out of doors. What had happened there? Presumably it was midday, and work in the fields had stopped. Stillness and quiet had replaced the previous animation. The birds had taken themselves off to feed in the brooks. The horses stood still. Yet the power was there all the same, massed outside indifferent, impersonal, not attending to anything in particular. Somehow it was opposed to the little hay-coloured moth. It was useless to try to do anything. One could only watch the extraordinary efforts made by those tiny legs against an oncoming doom which could, had it chosen, have submerged an entire city, not merely a city, but masses of human beings; nothing, I knew, had any chance against death. Nevertheless after a pause of exhaustion the legs fluttered again. It was superb this last protest, and so frantic that he succeeded at last in righting himself. One's sympathies, of course, were all on the side of life. Also, when there was nobody to care or to know, this gigantic effort on the part of an insignificant little moth, against a power of such magnitude, to retain what no one else valued or desired to keep, moved one strangely. Again, somehow, one saw life, a pure bead. I lifted the pencil again, useless though I knew it to be. But even as I did so, the unmistakable tokens of death showed themselves. The body relaxed, and instantly grew stiff. The struggle was over. The insignificant little creature now knew death. As I looked at the dead moth, this minute wayside triumph of so great a force over so mean an antagonist filled me with wonder. Just as life had been strange a few minutes before, so death was now as strange. The moth having righted himself now lay most decently and uncomplainingly composed. O yes, he seemed to say, death is stronger than I am.

Log Entry 7

Compare this essay to Dillard's. What likenesses do you see? What differences? Do the essays come to similar or different conclusions?

Building Your Course Portfolio

Read through your logs and think about the various activities you've done with this chapter on essay. Talk with your partner about how your understanding and appreciation of the Dillard essay have changed or deepened as you have looked at it from different angles, as you have talked, written about, and mapped or drawn your ideas.

- What new questions can you ask now?

- Which angles of vision gave you the most insight and the most pleasure as you worked with Annie Dillard's essay, "Death of a Moth"?

- What else can you say about your understanding of Woolf's essay?

Using your logs, the texts, your graphics, events in your own experience that you feel are relevant, write and/or draw your reflections. Use any form—essay, graphic, poem—to convey your own thoughts about the ideas of Dillard and Woolf.

After you have written or drawn this reflection, decide which pieces you have drafted for this study could become portfolio entries. After you have selected, revised, and polished them, include them in your course portfolio. Refer to Chapter 1 for full instructions on preparing the portfolio and for written, graphic, and performance options that you could develop.

Complete your course portfolio by writing a preface in which you introduce yourself and your work. Also include a final self-assessment in which you detail how well you have met your initial goals and what further goals you would like to achieve. Put this all together in a sturdy, attractive package of some sort and celebrate your growth in inquiring, comprehending, and composing.

Index of Authors and Titles

Credits *(continued from copyright page)*